FREEDOM, FOUCAULT, and the SUBJECT of AMERICA

FREEDOM, FOUCAULT, and the SUBJECT of AMERICA

Lee Quinby

BJ
352
Q56
1991

NORTHEASTERN UNIVERSITY PRESS   *Boston*

Northeastern University Press

Library of Congress Cataloging-in-Publication Data
Quinby, Lee, 1946–
    Freedom, Foucault, and the subject of America / Lee
    Quinby.
        p. cm.
    Includes bibliographical references and index.
    ISBN 1-55553-108-3 (alk. paper).
    1. Ethics—United States—History. 2. Liberty—History.
3. Foucault, Michel.   I. Title
BJ352.Q56   1991
170'.973—dc20   91-9577

Designed by Liz Doles

Composed in Bembo by BookMasters, Inc., Ashland,
Ohio. Printed and bound by The Maple Press, York, Pennsylvania. The paper is Sebago Antique, an acid-free sheet.

MANUFACTURED IN THE UNITED STATES OF AMERICA
96 95 94 93 92 91   5 4 3 2 1

For Tom Hayes

From the idea that the self is not given
to us, I think that there is only one
practical consequence: we have to
create ourselves as a work of art.
                    Michel Foucault
          "On the Genealogy of Ethics"

CONTENTS

ACKNOWLEDGMENTS

In writing this book I have benefitted from the help and support of many people. I owe much of my understanding of and continuing fascination with Jefferson and Thoreau to Lester Cohen and Leonard Neufeldt, in whose graduate classes at Purdue University I first confronted the issues central to the ethical tradition I explore. Patrick Bidelman's suggestions for early versions of several chapters helped redirect my thinking in important ways. Special thanks also go to Virgil Lokke; attending his weekly reading group for three years was a wonderful exercise in persistent critique. My friendship and intellectual collaboration with Irene Diamond began at Purdue as well. Our conversations over the years are reflected in many ways throughout the book.

Hobart and William Smith Colleges provided me time away from teaching to complete the manuscript. Students at the Colleges made teaching a lively engagement with the texts discussed here. Colleagues provided the kinds of encouragement and intellectual vitality that made me want to continue writing and revising. I especially wish to thank Eric Patterson, Dan O'Connell, Deborah Tall, Grant Holly, Jim Crenner, Craig Rimmerman, Susan Henking, and Dunbar Moodie in this regard. Daniel Singal generously read and commented on the entire manuscript in an earlier version.

Colleagues from other institutions have provided good counsel, in particular Barbara Harlow, Michael Holly, Malini Johar Schueller, and Ludmilla Jordanova. Julia Watson and Sidonie Smith offered helpful suggestions on the Kingston chapter. I also wish to thank Andrew Mandel, former editor at Northeastern University Press, whose brief but not uncritical involvement spurred needed revision. I am indebted to Deborah Kops, Editorial Director at Northeastern, who saw the manuscript through its final stages, and to Steven Mailloux and Mary Loeffelholz who, as readers, provided insightful suggestions for improvement. Martha Yager skillfully edited the manuscript.

I am deeply grateful to Mary Katherine Wainwright and Marie-France Etienne for their friendship over the years. Pep Quinby and Tom Quinby have been generous in so many ways that I can only begin to express my appreciation to them. My sons Michael Miller and Paul Miller grew up during the years I was working on this book. They helped nurture it and me throughout that time, and I am gratified by their pride in my writing.

This work is an ongoing dialogue with Tom Hayes. His unqualified emotional and intellectual support made it possible for me to complete it. He has been a kind and thoughtful reader, a patient listener, a critic in the best sense of the word, and a loving friend. It is a pleasure to dedicate this book to him.

FREEDOM, FOUCAULT, and the SUBJECT of AMERICA

INTRODUCTION

An American Aesthetics of Liberty

*T*his book identifies and analyzes a tradition of ethics in America that presents self-stylization as a practice of freedom. I call this ethics an *aesthetics of liberty*. This stylization of freedom promotes selfhood as an activity of artistic creation, writing as a means of self-culture, and the art of the self as a personal and civic virtue. An aesthetics of liberty has been and continues to be the chief means by which Americans challenge disciplinary power relations. The following chapters trace the evocation of the term *liberty* and the presentation of a poetics of self in certain key texts: Thomas Jefferson's *Notes on the State of Virginia*, Margaret Fuller's *Woman in the Nineteenth Century*, Henry David Thoreau's *Walden*, James Agee and Walker Evans's *Let Us Now Praise Famous Men*, Maxine Hong Kingston's *The Woman Warrior*, and June Jordan's *On Call*.

Although this ethics is not exclusively text-based—for self-stylization involves any number of forms—this is a book specifically about books that call for and enact an aesthetics of liberty. These texts are works of practical ethics, offering opinions and advice on how people seeking freedom might conduct themselves. As Michel Foucault has observed in regard to ancient Greek treatises that promote the art of the self, such texts have an "etho-poetic" function because they "enable individuals to question their own conduct, to watch over and give shape to it, and to shape themselves as ethical subjects" (*Use of Pleasure* 13).

The narrative of an American aesthetics of liberty begins with the statement of "self-evident" truths in the Declaration of Independence: "that all men are created equal, that they are endowed by their Creator with certain unalienable Rights, that among these are Life, Liberty and the pursuit of Happiness." Thomas

Jefferson is the discursive founder of this ethics: in addition to authoring the Declaration, he wrote *Notes on the State of Virginia*, the first American treatise presenting an aesthetics of liberty.[1] Subsequent writers in the American tradition of democratic liberty have drawn upon and modified the Jeffersonian stance, which takes as two of its stated objectives freedom from domination and freedom from "uniformity of opinion" (*Notes* 160). From the outset, this ethics opposed the dominant value system of colonial America. With the formation of the American nation-state, an aesthetics of liberty continued to serve as a counter-ethics, that is, as a challenge to prevailing ethical systems. Today this stylization of existence is one of the most important means of resisting contemporary restrictions on freedom.

Throughout this study, in order to explain ethics as a force field of power relations comprising competing technologies of selfhood, I have drawn from Foucault's discussion of technologies of the self, which permit "individuals to effect by their own means or with the help of others a certain number of operations on their own bodies and souls, thoughts, conduct, and way of being, so as to transform themselves in order to attain a certain state of happiness, purity, wisdom, perfection, or immortality" ("Technologies" 18).[2] I want to show how, as an ethics seeking to perpetuate and extend the liberty gained from the Revolution, an aesthetics of liberty emphasizes possibilities of personal freedom and self-determination. That is, this ethics promotes a technology of the self that focuses on the care of the self as an art of living and a style of liberty.

I also want to show how, as a practice, the care of the self resists technologies of normalization. By normalization I mean, again drawing from Foucault, those modes of power and their corresponding techniques and practices of self that discipline and regulate the body or soul, thus producing docility and conformity; that classify people as either "abnormal" or "normal," then segregate and punish or rehabilitate those deemed "abnormal"; and that define diverse people monolithically, that is, totalize a population in terms of national identity and eugenic obligation. Foucault calls these generative modes of body and population management the deployment of sexuality or bio-power.[3] I believe that, from its inception, the American ethics of an aesthetics of liberty has opposed not just these technologies of normalization but the desirability of normalization itself. That is, the very goals of normalization—uniformity of values and homogeneity of selfhood as prescribed by the law and the human sciences—are antithetical to an aesthetics of liberty. According to this ethics, practices of self-stylization might be shared, but they must not be prescribed. This is not to say that an aesthetics of liberty is devoid of danger to democratic freedom. No power relation is.

It is important to stress that the kinds of resistance that an aesthetics of liberty enacts in opposition to normalizing power relations are endemic to those power relations. This is the insight of Foucault's statement that "where there is power, there is resistance, and yet, or rather consequently, this resistance is never in a position of exteriority in relation to power" (*History of Sexuality* 95). Foucault's view has been sharply criticized by some engaged in contemporary critical debate over the issues with which this book is concerned, perhaps most notably Richard Rorty. In *Contingency, Irony, and Solidarity*, he argues that Foucault's line of thought, although "invaluable in our attempt to form a private self-image," is "pretty much useless when it comes to politics" (83). Rorty proposes a liberal utopia or " 'poeticized' culture . . . which has given up the attempt to unite one's private ways of dealing with one's finitude and one's sense of obligation to other human beings" (68). He argues that the "vocabulary of self-creation is necessarily private, unshared, unsuited to argument" and that the "vocabulary of justice is necessarily public and shared, a medium for argumentative exchange" (xiv). What I hope to demonstrate in this study, contra Rorty, is that ethical practices of freedom are necessarily involved in deliberation, dialogue, and struggle with oneself and with others. Such practices are simultaneously private and public, or, more accurately, they dislodge the private/public dichotomy altogether.

The impulse to define freedom through an aesthetics of liberty emerged from the struggle for a new nation and from an awareness of the investments of power integral to the emerging human sciences. The overthrow of monarchical authority and the decline of pastoral power made space for the authority of the human sciences. Such changes in modes of governance fueled concerns about the relationship between individuals and the state, simultaneously introducing two opposing possibilities: one of greater personal freedom and self-determination within American society and one of greater normalization and totalization of the population. These two possibilities recur as a major problematic in the texts I consider. In other words, America's ethical aesthetics of liberty emerged within and as part of the context of the modern era's normalizing bio-power and is therefore vitally engaged in questions concerning individual and national freedom produced by those power relations.

In America's aesthetics of liberty, the self that is being formed is assumed to be a work of art: not a work in which one becomes what one is "intended" to be, but a set of practices through which one questions the ways one has been formed as a subject.[4] Hence, beauty is considered a paramount ethical category. But, as I will show, shifts have occurred in the ways that beauty has been defined by proponents of this ethics. An inheritor of the presuppositions of the Enlightenment, Jefferson embraced the ancient Greek ideal of beauty as harmony even as he emphasized the disharmony of oppression. His attention to the effects of slavery on the moral and physical well-being of both slaves and slaveholders provides a case in point. In a chapter aptly called "Manners" in *Notes on the State of Virginia*, he observes that "there must doubtless be an unhappy influence on the manners of our people produced by the existence of slavery among us" and warns that "unremitting despotism on the one part, and degrading submissions on the other" kenneled the masters as well as the enslaved (162). Within the logic of this ethics, as here professed by a white slaveholder, the ideal of beauty necessitates the emancipation of slaves—for the sake of the masters

as much as for the sake of the slaves. For twentieth-century proponents like Kingston and Jordan, beauty remains an ethical category, but it is depicted less as a natural ideal to attain and more
as a means of critique of existing modes of subject formation.

Placing ethics within an aesthetic mode rather than a religious
or scientific one opposes the two major technologies of normalizing power/knowledge operating in America in the eighteenth
century: the long-entrenched power of the pastoral and the
newer bio-power of the human sciences. This is not to say that
aesthetics was previously outside either of these domains. For
Christianity incorporated a neoplatonic metaphysics in which
beauty was an absolute condition of the divine and integral to it.
But since art, particularly within Protestantism, was considered
the product of a lower material order, it was regarded as imita-
tive at best and deceptive at worst. When aesthetic or identifi-
ably expressive form appeared in Protestant discourse, as in the
majestic boldness of Edward Taylor's poetry, for example, it was
made subservient to the metaphysical message, because a love of
ornament threatened love of the divine. The human sciences also
located aesthetics within their own power/knowledge formations, separating aesthetics and ethics into two distinct philosophical subjects. This separation may be seen in the effort to
formalize aesthetics into an autonomous discipline focusing on
the philosophical rules of taste, as Alexander Baumgarten did
when he coined the term *aesthetics* in 1735.

Key differences between the technologies of the self within
America's technology of pastoral power and that of the human
sciences may be demonstrated by examining representative discourses of each. Exemplary of the relationship between truth and
selfhood in American Protestant ethics is Thomas Hooker's sermon "Meditation" (1659). Hooker defines meditation as "*a serious intention of the mind whereby wee come to search out the truth, and
settle it effectually upon the heart.*" In meditation, Hooker asserts,
one "beats his brain, . . . hammers out a business," or, in a more
poetic vein, makes a "meal of musing." But Hooker's sermon
also stresses the insufficiency of meditation for the attainment of

truth, for God alone bestows truth on the human soul. "The Goldsmith observes that it is not the laying of the fire," Hooker counsels, "but the blowing of it that melts the Mettal: So with Meditation, it breaths upon any Truth that is applied, and that makes it really sink and soak into the soul" (301–5). Were it not for God's bestowal of truth, then, there would be no fire upon which human meditation might breathe. In a discourse like Hooker's, truth is denominated as transcendent, that is, as absolute, immutable, eternal, and wholly Other, belonging to the domain of God. Divine revelation is the means by which the fires of grace are infused into one's spiritual self.

In contrast to the *self-renunciatory* imperatives of pastoral ethics, the technology of self operating within the human sciences stresses a set of practices geared toward *positively producing* a citizenry that might best serve the ends of government so that government might best serve its population. Benjamin Franklin's "bold and arduous Project of arriving at moral perfection" (66) provides one of the clearest and yet one of the most complex eighteenth-century examples of the human sciences' moral system, which promotes habit over revelation and regulation over submission to divine will. On the one hand, Franklin presents a completely externalized notion of self that is antithetical to Puritan conceptualizations of inner virtue. As Norman Fiering argues, "Franklin defended an essentially behaviorist approach to virtue, which paid little heed to purity of intention and inward renewal, but concentrated instead, on habit formation" (217). On the other hand, however, throughout the autobiography, Franklin's use of irony intimates that there is a self that may well differ from his virtuous persona, a self that he alone may know.

The tension between external and internal selfhood within Franklin's discourse is one that extends to the technology of the normalized self in general. But modern formations of bio-power "resolve" the tension by making the internal self increasingly visible through techniques of verbalization and thus more readily monitored. The logic of the external self manifest in Franklin's project for moral perfection was formalized a century later in philosophical utilitarianism's application of scientific method to morality, as found, for example, in Social Darwinism. This mode has achieved dominance in the twentieth century through the increasing authority of the apparatuses of normalization. This technology of power/knowledge largely informs the discourses of bourgeois medicine, psychology, economics, education, and politics and holds the view that truth is discernible in proportion to the completeness and rigor of gathered data. Franklin's ironic refusal to disclose his internal self has been overturned and supplanted by a mandate to "confess" the truth of one's self, a truth that becomes part of the classificatory data of the human sciences.

Jefferson departs dramatically from the ethical systems produced through both pastoral power relations and those of the human sciences. He posits an aesthetic self rather than an interiorist or behaviorist self. Unlike texts written in the pastoral mode, his writings do not subordinate the aesthetic to the divine. Nor do they follow the dominant Enlightenment practice of separating aesthetics and morality into two distinct disciplines. Quite the contrary: as the discussion in chapter 1 will demonstrate, Jefferson's writings stress the role to be played by literature, music, the visual arts, and architecture in the creation of an ethical life. One of Jefferson's most important departures from the ethics of both the pastoral and the human sciences is his insistence on uniting intellect, emotion, imagination, and the senses in order to promote virtue. The prominence that his discourse grants to the imagination contrasts dramatically with the Christian distrust of that faculty. And the elevated role of sentiment in his writings diverges from the human sciences' valorization of rationality over sentiment. It is precisely the belief in the vitality of rationality *and* sentiment, the sensory *and* the imaginary, that provides one of the points of resistance within America's aesthetics of liberty—that aesthetics and ethics are mutually constitutive.

In addition to challenging the dominant political-ethical systems of the time, Jefferson's aesthetic ethics diverges from the

prevailing characterization of aesthetic experience in his time—
and in ours as well. This divergence is related to the statuses of
beauty and sublimity. As Jerome Stolnitz has argued, during the
Enlightenment beauty lost its centrality within the general field
of aesthetics and came to be regarded as only one of several types
of aesthetic experience. Stolnitz points out that, in the aesthetic
theory of Edmund Burke, "beauty and sublimity are, conceptually, not only distinct but mutually exclusive" (191). The dimin-
ishment of beauty as an aesthetic category has been paralleled by
its devaluation as an ethical category.

Over the last two centuries, the sublime has grown increasingly central to both aesthetics and ethics. Postmodernism's
current fascination with the technological sublime reinscribes
Burke's dichotomy between the sublime and the beautiful, to the
detriment of an aesthetics of liberty. While the sublime is a compelling description of the overwhelming confusion wrought by
technological simulation and hyperspace, the corresponding relegation of beauty to an inferior status propels political-ethical
discourse away from possibilities of resistance and toward a Bau-
drillardian logic of postmodern apocalypse. This is not to say
that the depiction of beauty as an ethical category is unproblem-
atic. As Nazi Germany's uses of beauty indicate, when beauty is
defined in terms of order and harmony derived from the suppression of differences and conflicting voices, then it is totalitarian. This is why the discourses of America's aesthetics of liberty
so often use the sublime as a force of conceptual resistance to
beauty made static. They seek to disrupt the definition of beauty
as perpetual order.

In contrast to Burke and his postmodern disciples, Jefferson
conceptualized the sublime as necessary to beauty. The differences between Burke's view and Jefferson's involve a politics of
gender as well as a politics of resistance. As W. J. T. Mitchell has
pointed out, for Burke "sublimity, with its foundations in pain,
terror, vigorous exertion, and power, is the masculine aesthetic
mode. Beauty, by contrast, is located in qualities such as little-
ness, smoothness, and delicacy that mechanically induce a sense

of pleasure and affectionate superiority" (129). Although Jefferson's metaphors of sublimity and beauty concur with Burke's gender designations of the sublime as masculine and the beautiful as feminine, he reverses Burke's hierarchy of sexual difference by portraying sublimity as the force necessary for revolution and beauty as the attainment of freedom. Whereas Jefferson retained a gender differentiation in regard to male and female citizenry, Margaret Fuller problematized such a differentiation. Twentieth-century proponents of aesthetic ethics, while perpetuating Jefferson's association of the sublime with immensely powerful and disruptive forces and the beautiful with freedom and happiness, followed Fuller in according men and women equality in civic responsibility.

The use of the secular sublime as a means to beauty appears throughout the texts I see formulating an aesthetics of liberty. Many of these texts have an ecological dimension in which sublimity and beauty are associated with nature. Sublimity represents the available energies of both the American landscape and its people; beauty, the possibilities of democratic freedom. From Jefferson, Fuller, and Thoreau to Wendell Berry, Annie Dillard, and Edward Abbey, one finds depictions of heightened senses and emotions in response to terror-inducing spaces of nature. These writers issue warnings about the depletion of the land at the hands of those who would merely exploit or ravage it. Their writings seek to preserve the sublime as a resource for individuals and the nation.

While some aesthetic-ethical writers treat America's landscape as an emblem of the sublime that makes beauty possible—as a literal as well as figurative space for the grounding of liberty—others accentuate the sublime and the beautiful in relation to dynamics among and within people. In *Woman in the Nineteenth Century*, for example, Fuller associates sublimity with masculine energy and beauty with feminine form to argue that artistry of self and society require both. Throughout *Walden*, Thoreau uses the "wild" as a form of the sublime and the "chaste" as a form of the beautiful to argue that the wild provides a "generative energy" that is necessary for aesthetic-ethical development. Similarly, in his apocalyptic *Fire Next Time,* James Baldwin warns that fiery forces of revolutionary energy among blacks will be used if necessary to convince the white world of the beauty of the black world. Thus, the representation of the sublime as a social force may be seen as a carnivalization of the dominant social order. It is a suspension of normalizing discipline—a terror-inducing disruption of the hierarchies of hegemonic power/knowledge—which makes possible a different social order.

Whether attributed to nature, personal experience, or society, the sublime and the beautiful are represented in these writings as vehicles for social and personal transformation; that is, the disruptive sublime is seen as making possible individual and civic beauty. In other words, according to this conceptualization of ethics, one combats normalizing and regulatory mechanisms of discipline through exercises of self-stylization understood as a means of acquiring truths that are to be transformed into action. By portraying America as a society in the process of being created as a work of art—and themselves and others as creators—these writers stress the artistic and ethical potential of individuals and society. Thus, in America's aesthetics of liberty, beauty is not a given; this is not an anesthetized aesthetic. It is a changing artistic activity of self and society, an activity made possible by disruptive energies conceived of as the sublime.

In its regard for the created self and its use of beauty as an ethical category, America's aesthetics of liberty challenges assumptions of both pastoral power's technology of the renounced self and the human sciences' technology of the normalized self. Although such an ethics neither (necessarily) denies the metaphysical nor disregards the empirical, it forwards concepts of selfhood and truth defined as acts of human creation rather than as revelation or discovery. Instead of proposing either prayer or scientific method as the proper means of discerning moral direction, writers of America's aesthetics of liberty posit exercises in the art of living, including reading, physical training, and writing, as guides for ethical and political conduct. In keeping with the premises of contextualized truths and beauty, a number of rhetorical practices tend to recur among these writers: an insistence that ethics and aesthetics are interrelated and mutually constitutive; an attention to the sublimity and beauty of nature and humanity and to the etho-poetic potential of both; an appropriation of a religious idiom for describing the physical-cultural world; an exhortation to become artists of self, of the landscape, and of society; and a disclosure of the great difficulty of those tasks.

The works considered here have been chosen for their roles both in fostering an aesthetics of liberty and in resisting proliferating forces of normalizing bio-power within their particular historical moments. That resistance is formulated through what Foucault refers to as a "problemization by thought." "Thought is not," he argues, "what inhabits a certain conduct and gives it its meaning; rather, it is what allows one to step back from this way of acting or reacting, to present it to oneself as an object of thought and question it as to its meaning, its conditions, and its goals. Thought is freedom in relation to what one does, the motion by which one detaches oneself from it, establishes it as an object, and reflects on it as a problem" ("Polemics, Politics, and Problemizations" 388).

This concept of thought redefines the intellectual tradition in America that espouses transcendent Truth. It formulates the place of the intellectual as dialogical and specific rather than prophetic and universal. The texts I have selected for discussion are especially rich in this regard because of the way they situate themselves in relation to other texts, respond to themes introduced by other intellectuals (particularly by Jefferson), and overtly oppose claims for transcendent Truth. In moving from Jefferson to Jordan, we see a shift from what Gramsci calls the *organic intellectual* to what Foucault calls the *specific intellectual*. This is a shift from a model of revolution to a model of resistances. As Andrew Ross has shown, both models run counter to the ideal of a *universal intellectual* who is believed to have access to transcendental principles (213–32). But as we move from Gramsci to Foucault, and from Jefferson to Jordan, we can also trace a critique of the totalizing model of *the* revolution. In place of a single, unified transformation, the notion of resistances emphasizes local, partial, often contradictory strategies for change. One of the goals of this study, then, is to show the ways in which increased specificity—not universality—is necessary for thinking through contemporary issues of global importance, such as the AIDS crisis, ecological destruction, nuclear arms, and poverty.

My focus on the six works discussed here is, of course, not exhaustive of this radical ethical tradition in America. These pages might have been devoted to works by Ralph Waldo Emerson, Frederick Douglass, Harriet Jacobs, Walt Whitman, William James, Emma Goldman, Jane Addams, John Dewey, James Baldwin, Vine Deloria, Gloria Anzaldúa—and others.[5] I do not mean to suggest that this tradition of ethics has been a unified or a teleological development of the idea of freedom. I have selected texts that allow me to demonstrate that the textual forms of America's aesthetics of liberty have been discontinuous, aimed at specific targets, and necessarily changing. Hence this study has been "arranged" insofar as I have chosen texts for their problemization of certain assumptions found in predecessor texts.

I am especially interested in the three technologies of power/ knowledge most constitutive of American subjectivity—namely the family, education, and sexuality—their localization in the body, and their relationship to the law. My readings focus on the ways these six texts have reassessed these technologies in keeping with an aesthetics of liberty. Through such problemizations by thought, they have promoted the freedom of the subject and extended the subject of freedom. In my readings of them I have tried to do the same.

In the first chapter I will discuss Thomas Jefferson's inauguration of an American aesthetics of liberty in *Notes on the State of Virginia* as a problemization of colonial practices of self. I argue that *Notes* advocates a pursuit of happiness defined as an ethical category of beauty so vital as to justify the Revolution and guide the establishment of the new nation. Subsequent chapters show how an ethical aesthetics of liberty has, over the last two centuries, been the discourse of intellectuals who, like Jefferson, have problematized existing concepts of freedom, selfhood, beauty, and ethical conduct for Americans.

Chapters 2 and 3 focus on the different ways that Margaret Fuller and Henry David Thoreau challenge the proliferation in the nineteenth century of the normalized, sexualized subject of desire. I argue that their writings participate in what Foucault called a "movement of desexualisation." In opposition to the normalizing deployment of sexuality, their texts displace that deployment's sexual centering of identity and conduct. Such desexualization looks for "new forms of community, coexistence, pleasure" ("The Confession of the Flesh" 219–20). In her *Woman in the Nineteenth Century*, Fuller contests what was, in her time, the received notion of virtue, a notion that replicated the prejudice of its Latin derivation—from *vir* for man—in assuming virtue to be the special prerogative of men. Her concept of gender aesthetics desexualizes the female self not only by depicting women in the process of becoming etho-poetic subjects but also by showing how that process is necessary if men are to achieve virtue. Chapter 3's discussion of Thoreau's appropriation of the concept of chastity indicates the ways in which *Walden* challenges the dominant ethics and power mechanisms of the antebellum era by desexualizing the male subject of desire. The sexualized male subject is produced in the nexus of the family, whereby sons become fathers, and in industrial capitalism, whereby fathers become breadwinners.

The last three chapters focus on writings that foster an aesthetics of liberty in the twentieth century, an era of proliferating mechanisms of normalizing power/knowledge and intensifying national imperialism. James Agee and Walker Evans draw on a notion of human divinity in *Let Us Now Praise Famous Men* to expose poverty as a condition caused by America's socioeconomic system and rationalized through disciplinary formations of surveillance. Evans's photographs use iconoclastic imagery and Agee's text uses metaphors and techniques of film and music in order to destabilize univocal meaning systems and claims of unitary, objective reality. Their challenges to governmental and human-sciences surveillance foster a practice of self-stylization that refuses to objectify the Other.

The last two chapters focus on the works of two contemporary intellectuals whose writings from the margins demand a decentering of hegemonic power/knowledge. In chapter 5 I discuss the ways in which Maxine Hong Kingston's *The Woman Warrior* both challenges the model of unified subjectivity produced in traditional autobiography and promotes a form of ideographic selfhood. Her formulation of an aesthetics of liberty extends and problematizes Fuller's and Thoreau's explorations of sexuality and gender as well as Agee's and Evans's critiques of representation. The concluding chapter turns explicitly to the role of the specific intellectual in the contemporary era, discussing June Jordan's deconstruction of imperialistic models of language, literature, and politics. Jordan's writings demonstrate how acting as a specific intellectual is itself a practice of freedom and self-stylization.

In each case, the literary merit of these texts has been generally acknowledged, though not without a struggle in the academic literary arena. But the texts have been pushed to the margins of the American philosophical and political canons.[6] This has been possible because of the separation of aesthetics, ethics, and politics into discrete disciplines. Furthermore, all of these disciplines tend to be regarded as areas of study separated or abstracted from everyday life. This book is an effort to redress that disciplinary separation and marginalization by showing how these texts are a practical ethics and an ethical practice for writers composing their lives as works of art. Taken together, these texts constitute a profound contribution to the freedom of the American subject.

CHAPTER ONE

Securing the Freedom of the Subject: Jefferson's *Notes on the State of Virginia* and the State of Happiness

I have no more made my book than my book has made me," declares Montaigne in his *Essays*, which he describes as "a book consubstantial with its author, concerned with my own self, an integral part of my life" (2: 18, 504). Montaigne's notion of essaying as an act of self-composition may be seen as a benchmark of America's aesthetics of liberty, for his ethics presents itself as an assaying or testing of ideas in writing that is itself an act of self-creation. This idea of self-authorization, of writing oneself into existence rather than finding one's core self from deep within the recesses of either the soul or the unconscious, challenges the technologies of power and the self predominating in the modern era. Montaigne not only renounces the right of pastoral and human-science authorities to prescribe confessional normalizing methods for deciphering "inner" selfhood, he proposes an ethics in which aesthetics is the overriding principle through which the individual self is created. What Foucault has said about the aesthetics of existence practiced by the ancient Greeks applies to Montaigne and to American artists of liberty as well. All have deemed "writing for oneself and for others" an *askesis*, or exercise, through which one can learn "the art of living" ("Genealogy" 245–51). Writing as an *askesis*, Foucault argues, is "the living substance of philosophy, . . . an exercise of oneself in the activity of thought" (*Use of Pleasure* 9).

Just as the writing of the Declaration of Independence was part of the process of inventing America as a nation and Thomas

Jefferson as a statesman (see Gary Wills, *Inventing America*), the writing of *Notes on the State of Virginia* was part of the process of creating Virginia as a state and its author as an ethical subject of freedom. But Jefferson's views—despite his appropriation as a founding father of bourgeois values—have never been part of the dominant ethos in America. Richard Matthews argues that Jefferson's "humanism, his communitarian anarchism, and his radical democracy make his political views stand as an alternative to the market liberalism of the past and present" (122). It is in this capacity—as an alternative always pushed to the margins of the American ideological text—that *Notes on the State of Virginia* may be seen as the inaugural discourse of an American ethics of an aesthetics of liberty.

In this chapter I will read Jefferson's depiction of Virginia as a trope for an aesthetic-ethical self. His equations between the state of Virginia and the state of happiness of Virginians and Americans introduce a new concept of selfhood, a post-Revolutionary ethos prompted by the radical rupture between England and America. This new self is a subject-in-process: working for the democratic well-being of Virginia is a way of becoming a subject of liberty. By associating Virginia and its citizenry in this way, *Notes* establishes an ethos that links personal virtue with civic virtue.[1]

The state of being toward which *Notes* shows the state of Virginia to be moving is one that Jefferson proclaimed often, in public documents and private letters, to be the "aim of life": happiness (letter to William Short, Oct. 31, 1819).[2] No doubt Jefferson's most famous pronouncement of the right to pursue happiness is the one in the Declaration of Independence. But this view was not new for him in 1776. As early as 1763 he had written to John Page that "perfect happiness I believe was never intended by the deity to be the lot of any one of his creatures in this world; but that he had very much put in our power the nearness of our approaches to it, is what I as steadfastly believe" (July 15, 1763). Jefferson reiterated this view throughout his life. In 1782, for example, he wrote that "the giver of life . . . gave it for happiness and not for wretchedness" (to Monroe, May 20, 1782). And in a letter to Ezra Stiles, Jefferson defended Shays' Rebellion, observing that "if the happiness of the mass of people can be secured at the expense of a little tempest now and then, or even a little blood, it will be a precious purchase" (Dec. 24, 1786).

In *Notes*, the concept of a happiness founded upon virtuous self-stylization, gauged through utility, and experienced as pleasurable tranquillity introduces a technology of the self that is opposed to the modern era's subject of desire. This subject, Foucault has shown, derived initially from Christian confessional practices and later, during the Enlightenment, from practices of normalization in the family, the school, the prison, the military, and the clinic. Since Jefferson's day, the promise of fulfillment for the desiring subject has come to be equated with happiness. But for the desiring subject happiness remains forever a promise. As Juliet Flower MacCannell observes about the dynamics of post-Enlightenment society, "the machine of culture is literally *driven* by the excess of desire over satisfaction" (936). Within the practices of normalization, the desiring subject seeks a truth of self that must *always* be deferred, pursues a desire that can *never* be satisfied. Such a subjectivity—so integral to a capitalist society—is resisted in *Notes* through an aesthetics of liberty in which happiness is depicted as attainable through self-creating practices that simultaneously create a democratic society.

Jefferson's aesthetics of liberty draws from both ancient and contemporary moral discourses, in particular those of Epicurus, Epictetus, Jesus, and the Moral Sense School.[3] In *Notes*, the ancient classical and Christian philosophies complement one another despite their traditional differences. This complementarity is made plausible by Jefferson's antimetaphysical view of Jesus and by his adaptation of the Moral Sense School's coupling of aesthetics and morality. Nowhere in *Notes*, however, are these philosophies cited as moral guides. A likely reason for this appears in the letter Jefferson wrote to Benjamin Rush when he shared his syllabus of the doctrines of Jesus with him: Jefferson

expressed confidence that, with Rush, the syllabus would "not
be exposed to the malignant perversions of those who make
every word from me a text for new misrepresentations and cal-
umnies. I am moreover averse to the communication of my religious tenets to the public; . . . it behooves every man who values
liberty of conscience for himself, to resist invasions of it in the
case of others" (April 21, 1803).[4] A declaration of allegiance to
Epicurus would have posed an equal if not greater political and
personal risk, given the common misperception of Epicureanism
as equivalent to hedonism. Jefferson hinted at such a risk in an
after-dinner conversation in 1807, when he remarked to John
Quincy Adams that "the *Epicurean* philosophy came nearest to
the truth . . . of any ancient system of philosophy, but that it has
been misunderstood and misrepresented" (Adams 472).

In a letter to William Short, Jefferson was equally laudatory
about the precepts of Epicurus and Epictetus. "As you say of
yourself, I too am an Epicurian," he wrote. "I consider the gen-
uine (not the imputed) doctrines of Epicurus as containing everything rational in moral philosophy which Greece and Rome have
left us. Epictetus indeed, has given us what was good of the
Stoics; all beyond, of their dogmas, being hypocrisy and gri-
mace." To this letter Jefferson attached a syllabus of the doctrines
of Epicurus that he had put together "some twenty years ago."
Written in "lapidary style," the syllabus outlines the moral doctrines of Epicurus and places happiness in conceptual opposition
to desire and fear:

> Happiness the aim of life.
> Virtue the foundation of happiness.
> Utility the test of Virtue.
> Pleasure active and In–do–lent.
> In–do–lence is the absence of pain, the true felicity.
> Active, consists in agreeable motion; it is not happiness, but
>   the means to produce it.
> Thus the absence of hunger is an article of felicity; eating the
>   means to obtain it.

> The *summum bonum* is to be not pained in body, nor troubled in mind.
>
> i.e. In-do-lence of body, tranquillity of mind.
>
> To procure tranquillity of mind we must avoid desire and fear, the two principle diseases of the mind.
>
> Man is a free agent.
>
> Virtue consists in 1. Prudence. 2. Temperance. 3. Fortitude. 4. Justice.
>
> To which are opposed, 1. Folly. 2. Desire. 3. Fear. 4. Deceit. (Oct. 31, 1819)

Jefferson evaluated the relative merits of the classical and Christian philosophies in his 1803 letter to Rush. The precepts of the ancient philosophers, he wrote, "related chiefly to ourselves, and the government of those passions which, unrestrained, would disturb our tranquillity of mind." These teachings were deficient, however, in "developing our duties to others. . . . Still less have they inculcated peace, charity and love to our fellow men, or embraced with benevolence the whole family of mankind." By contrast, Jesus, who "was meek, benevolent, patient, firm, disinterested, and of the sublimest eloquence," gave doctrines "relating to kindred and friends" that "were more pure and perfect than those of the most correct of the philosophers." His teachings "inculcat[ed] universal philanthropy, not only to kindred and friends, to neighbors and countrymen, but to all mankind, gathering all into one family, under the bonds of love, charity, peace, common wants and common aids" (April 21, 1803). Some years after writing to Rush, Jefferson repeated this view to Short, stating succinctly that "Epictetus and Epicurus give laws for governing ourselves, Jesus a supplement of the duties and charities we owe to others" (Oct. 31, 1819).

Moral Sense philosophy helped Jefferson address these issues by providing him with an Enlightenment-style blend of the classical and the Christian.[5] This philosophy was informed by Greek ethics in three key ways. First, it emphasized the ancient Greek definition of good conduct as aesthetic harmony. Second, it taught the compatibility of personal virtue with civic virtue. And third, it took up the Epicurean belief in utility as a gauge of morality. These principles marked a break from Christianity's postulation of an absolute and universal morality. Upon them, however, Moral Sense philosophy grafted a different universal: benevolence. The moral sense, held to be innate, made benevolence toward one's countrymen possible. Such a view was a form of humanist Christianity, rejecting Calvinist concepts of innate depravity and predestination.

"The Creator would indeed have been a bungling artist," Jefferson wrote in 1814, "had he intended man for a social animal, without planting in him social dispositions." It is because of our social dispositions, our moral sense, that "good acts give us pleasure." There is a "want or imperfection of the moral sense in some men," however, and education and benevolent laws "serve to supply the defect" as well as to cultivate the moral sense in those in whom it is not found wanting. Development of the moral sense is crucial, Jefferson argues, because there is no single definition of virtue, and, for that reason, "nature has constituted *utility* to man, the standard test of virtue. Men living in different countries, under different circumstances, different habits and regimens, may have different utilities; the same act, therefore, may be useful, and consequently virtuous in one country which is injurious and vicious in another differently circumstanced" (letter to Law, June 13, 1814). Virtue useful in a given country, Jefferson suggests, will be experienced as happiness: the pleasurable tranquillity that results from personal and social harmony.

Jefferson's blending of classical and Christian principles should be viewed in the context of the changing material and philosophical conditions accompanying the formation of the nation-state. Rapid cultural changes stemming from the growing burdens of colonization, the diminishing powers of the monarchy, and the proliferating mass media necessitated rethinking of the principles of citizenship. To the extent that Jefferson's ethics drew on the ancient Greek model, it accentuated the individual's relationship to self, a relationship defined but not determined by society. But to the extent that it drew from Moral Sense philosophy, with the notion of a benevolence shared by the nation, it accorded with a political technology that subsumed individuality within the requirements of society.

This tension between the individual and the state is not resolved in Jefferson's work or, for that matter, in subsequent American works promoting an aesthetics of liberty. It is, rather, formulated as a problematic to be struggled with, a set of inquiries about how one is to be both personally ethical and socially responsible. All of the writings under study here focus on this problematic, dealing with it in different ways, under different historical and cultural circumstances. For Jefferson and for subsequent writers of America's aesthetics of liberty, the problematic focuses most intensely on the relationship between the law and the technologies of sexuality, the family, and education—all sites of power where freedom has been denied to racial and ethnic minorities, women, and the poor. *Notes* offers a way of addressing these issues by formulating a subjectivity and a concept of truth that are always in a process of creation and thereby resist codification and regulation.

To argue that the ethics proposed in *Notes* resists the modern era's technologies of normalization, then, is not to suggest that the work transcends its historical conditions. Both the Declaration and *Notes* argue, for example, that humanity's happiness is part of the grand design of God and nature; hence, they espouse the traditional presumptions of the Enlightenment about nature's harmonious totality, the deistic design of the universe, and humanity's innate moral sense. Furthermore, Jefferson's ethics manifests racist, sexist, and elitist assumptions, as seen in his bias toward blacks as physically and mentally less "beautiful" than whites and his view that the domestic sphere is the proper domain for women's happiness. Also, his contempt for the poor is evident: "The mobs of great cities add just so much to the support of pure government, as sores do to the strength of the human body" (*Notes* 165). Such attitudes show that an ethics based on aesthetics is not inherently free of its era's oppressive assumptions about the "natural" and the "superior." But in the case of *Notes*, an ethics based on an aesthetics of liberty provided Americans with a way of resisting not only the powers that had colonized them but also those that would normalize them.

L ike Montaigne's *Essays, Notes on the State of Virginia* is a work "consubstantial with its author," a work that demonstrates the ways in which writing that expresses an aesthetics of liberty is an activity of self-creation for its author.[6] In 1780, on receiving a questionnaire circulated by François Marbois, secretary of the French legation in Philadelphia, Jefferson undertook the project of disseminating information about Virginia to the French government. Most of the original work was written during the final months of his disastrous term as governor of Virginia, while the state was under British siege, and shortly after his retirement, an equally dark period for him, which included an official inquiry by the Virginia legislature into his conduct as governor, a period of convalescence following a fall from a horse, the death of his infant daughter, and the ill health of his wife. In December of 1781, Jefferson sent his commentaries to Marbois. Apparently dissatisfied with the work and perhaps drawing sustenance from the act of writing, he began revisions shortly thereafter, continuing over the years in which his wife died (1782) and he participated in the Continental Congress. After sharing his work with friends and making further revisions in response to their suggestions, Jefferson decided to have the manuscript, now "swelled nearly to treble bulk" (letter to Chastellux, Jan. 16, 1784), printed for private distribution while he was in France negotiating with European allies. This edition, which was completed in May 1785 and totaled 200 copies, appeared under the title *Notes on the State of Virginia*, without Jefferson's name. Pressed for wider publication in France and concerned about the threat of pirated editions, Jefferson agreed to a French edition; this version, a poor translation filled with errors, appeared in 1787 with only his initial on the title page. Jefferson then decided to authorize an English edition based on the private one of 1785. This 1787 Stockdale edition was the first on which his name appeared and in which he stated (in the "Advertisement") that the "FOL-LOWING NOTES" were "now offered to the public."

With the Stockdale edition, Jefferson officially became the author of *Notes on the State of Virginia*, but for him the act of authoring was by no means over: closure is the antithesis of writing as *askesis*, the progressive consideration of self, which is a process of acquiring and assimilating truth as a function of self-creation. As the annotations and additions in his personal copy of *Notes* indicate, this process—like his many remodelings of Monticello—lasted throughout his life. Although Jefferson reported at various intervals his intention to publish a new edition, in 1814 he wrote to a publisher that the "work itself indeed is nothing more than the measure of a shadow, never stationary, but lengthening as the sun advances, and to be taken anew from hour to hour. It must remain, therefore, for some other hand to sketch its appearance at another epoch, to furnish another element for calculating the course and motion of this member of our federal system" (to John Melish, Dec. 10, 1814). Even after bequeathing to others the preparation of a new edition, he continued to make notations and revisions in his own copy.

Given the number of years spent writing and revising his only book, one is led to wonder why Jefferson retained its "unpretentious title" (Peden xvi), despite the advice of his friend Charles Thomson. "[Y]ou . . . owe it to your reputation to publish your work under a more dignified title," Thomson wrote to Jefferson (March 6, 1785). Jefferson's reply, as Peden notes, did not accord with the amount of time devoted to *Notes*. "In literature nothing new," he wrote, "for I do not consider as having added any thing to that feild [*sic*] my own Notes of which I have had a few copies printed" (letter to Thomson, June 21, 1785). Yet the title *Notes* is as suggestive as that of Montaigne's *Essays* if one considers its range of meanings. Following the entries in the *OED*, we find that a note is first associated with music, as a written character and as a tone of musical sound. Second, it is defined as a mark that distinguishes a thing, ranging from a mark of high distinction, including theological election, to a mark of reproach or censure, to a sign of punctuation in writing and printing. Third, it is associated with legal records, particularly in regard to the transfer of land; with writing, done either to assist the memory in making a subsequent, more complete statement, or as a commentary on other writing; a bill of account, a short letter, or a formal diplomatic communication; and then with payment, as a receipt or promissory note. And finally the *OED* defines *note* in relation to the term "of note," as of distinction, importance, reputation, fame. As a lyrical tribute to Virginia, an empirical description of its physical and sociopolitical features, a record of the legal transfer of lands that constituted the state, a commentary on others' writings about it, a promissory note of future freedom, and a work of enduring reputation for its author, *Notes* is felicitously titled.

In structuring *Notes*, Jefferson rearranged the topics of Marbois's twenty-two queries into twenty-three chapters to match the classificatory system of his private library (Quinby 343–49). More significantly, he structured *Notes* to accord with an ethics in which aesthetics plays a crucial role. As he states in his 1815 Library Catalogue, "BOOKS may be classed according to the faculties of the mind employed on them: these are—I. MEMORY. II. REASON. III. IMAGINATION Which are applied respectively to—I. HISTORY. II. PHILOSOPHY. III. FINE ARTS" (Sowerby 13, no. 1258). However, while this categorization of knowledge corresponds to the traditional Baconian divisions of faculties of mind, the ranking of these faculties so as to privilege imagination and the fine arts was a radical departure from eighteenth-century religious authority. Jonathan Edwards, for example, warned that the "imagination or phantasy seems to be that wherein are formed all those delusions of Satan, which those are carried away with, who are under the influence of false religion, and counterfeit graces and affections. Here is the devil's grand lurking place, the very nest of foul and delusive spirits" (288).

Although most eighteenth-century secular writers took a less suspicious stance toward the workings of imagination, their writings generally ranked reason over imagination. By contrast, Jefferson held that "we are . . . wisely framed to be as warmly interested for a fictitious as for a real personage. The spacious field of imagination is thus laid open to our use, and lessons may be formed to illustrate and carry home to the mind every moral rule of life" (letter to Robert Skipwith, Aug. 3, 1771). *Notes* demonstrates in both form and content Jefferson's conviction that imagination and the arts are essential for cultivating virtue and attaining happiness.

In following Jefferson's library classification system from History to Philosophy to Fine Arts, the structure of *Notes* presents Virginia, and by extension America, anthropomorphically, as a self developing through the life stages of childhood, young adulthood, and maturity. The childhood stage (chapters 1–12) provides Virginia with a body, a past, and memory: resources to draw upon in the present and future. Jefferson begins this stage with Natural History instead of Civil History, reversing their places at the head of the Catalogue to suit his logic of development. The chapters on Civil History present Virginia's Age of Reason (late childhood), when mind emerges developmentally from body: Virginia reaches rationality through revolutionary struggle. The second (young adult) stage (chapters 13–22) deals with the philosophical Virginia of Jefferson's day, in which mental agility is developed. These chapters describe the creation of a social order and a revolutionary government, detailing legal, educational, and economic institutions. *Notes* was first published during this second state of Virginia's development, hence Jefferson's great concern with the preparatory practices guiding Virginians toward ethical citizenry. The third stage (chapter 23), which contains a discussion and listing of writings about Virginia from its founding through freedom and independence, points to a future of artistic maturity. The structure of each chapter, consisting of a "Query" and a response, suggests that a dialogic approach to knowledge is a feature of the maturation process itself. (Hereafter I follow Jefferson in calling his chapters "queries.")

Thus the work begins with subjects assigned by Jefferson's Catalogue to the mental faculty of memory, proceeds to those listed under reason, and ends with subjects classified as fine arts (rhetoric and bibliography). If one were to place *Notes* within this system of classification, it would belong with the fine arts as well, under "polygraphical," where one finds the works of "authors who have written on various branches."

In Query VI, Jefferson makes explicit his organic model of development and its culmination in happiness: "As in philosophy and war, so in government, in oratory, in painting, in the plastic art, we might shew that America, though but a child of yesterday, has already given hopeful proofs of genius, as well of the nobler kinds, which arouse the best feelings of man, which call him into action, which substantiate his freedom, and conduct him to happiness, as of the subordinate, which serve to amuse him only" (64–65). America, then, has reached an age of independence in art and science that enables it to attain happiness. How was this stage of independence achieved? That is the story of the first twelve queries.

Jefferson's topographical survey of Virginia accentuates its points of physical superiority to England and the other American states. In Query I, where he names the latitudes and longitudes that mark the boundaries of Virginia, Jefferson remarks, "This state is therefore one third larger than the islands of Great Britain and Ireland" (4). The colonial "child" thus exceeds the "parent" in physical stature. As Query II indicates, Virginia is the center of an extensive river system flowing to other states, territories, and nations. And, as Query IV claims, Virginia's mountain ranges, which "are not solitary and scattered confusedly over the face of the country" (18), make it "the spine of the country between the Atlantic on one side, and the Missisipi and St. Laurence on the other" (19). Thus, Jefferson *embodies* Virginia by presenting an analogy between its physical attributes and an ethics that defines the individual in developmental and interdependent terms: Virginia is to America as the arteries and spine are to the body.

Jefferson's metaphors for Virginia's corporal selfhood include a process of individuation from parental authority. In Query IV he describes the forces of the Potomac and the Shenandoah rivers rushing against the Blue Ridge mountain ranges as "monuments of a war" (20). If we follow the implication of his metaphor, this passage becomes a political allegory celebrating the colonial victory of independence over the mountainous British empire. Jefferson invites his readers to revel in nature's enactment of revolutionary independence. "You stand on a very high point of land," he writes:

> On your right comes up the Shenandoah, having ranged along the foot of mountain an hundred miles to seek a vent. On your left approaches the Patowmac, in quest of a passage also. In the moment of their junction they rush together against the mountain, rend it asunder, and pass off to the sea. The first glance of this scene hurries our senses into the opinion, that this earth has been created in time, that the mountains were formed first, that the rivers began to flow afterwards, that in this place particularly they have been dammed up by the Blue ridge of mountains, and have formed an ocean which filled the whole valley; that continuing to rise they have at length broken over at this spot, and have torn the mountain down from its summit to its base. (19)

These "monuments of a war" between forces of nature, he suggests, will—like the actual war between America and Great Britain—be to the benefit of Virginia and the new nation.

The aesthetic dynamic of this passage leads us from sublimity to beauty, for Jefferson follows the description of nature's vigorous warring forces with a scene of tranquillity.

> [T]he distant finishing which nature has given to the picture is of a very different character. It is a true contrast to the fore-ground.

It is as placid and delightful, as that is wild and tremendous. For
the mountain being cloven asunder, she presents to your eye,
through a cleft, a small catch of smooth blue horizon, at an infinite distance in the plain country, inviting you, as it were, from
the riot and tumult roaring around, to pass through the breach
and participate of the calm below. (19)

Implying that nature foretells peace and progress for Virginia, he
writes: "Here the eye ultimately composes itself; and that way
too the road happens actually to lead" (19).

Part of the drama of this often-anthologized passage derives
from its use of traditional gender categories that associate the
sublime with masculinity and the beautiful with femininity. Unlike Edmund Burke, however, who formalized these gender associations and privileged the sublime over the beautiful (Mitchell
129), Jefferson depicts warring "masculine" forces of sublimity as
the means by which "feminine" beauty is attained, encapsulating
in that sequence the developmental logic of his aesthetics of liberty. The politics of gender at work in Jefferson's model of aesthetics, in which beauty is made possible through sublime
disruptions, contrasts with the patriarchal politics of suppression
of the feminine in aesthetics, a suppression that contributes to the
subordination of women in society. In Jefferson's aesthetics of
liberty, feminine beauty is associated with civilization, which, in
regard to gender, he defines in separate-but-equal terms, stating
that it is "civilization alone which replaces women in the enjoy-
ment of their natural equality" (60). Thus, although Jefferson resists the definition of the "feminine" as a lack—his concept of
"feminine" beauty suggests a plenitude of virtue and happiness—
he regards women's "femininity" as disqualifying them for full
rights of citizenship. As the next chapter will demonstrate, Margaret Fuller problemizes the assumptions and the practices of this
gender-differentiated aesthetics of liberty.

Jefferson's description of the Natural Bridge in Query V recapitulates the movement from the sublime to the beautiful. The
passage begins with statistics to provide the reader with scien-

tific measurement, shifts to the pain and terror of the sublime, and concludes with a paean to the beautiful.[7] Upon walking to the side of the bridge, Jefferson reports, "You involuntarily fall on your hands and feet, creep to the parapet and peep over it. Looking down from this height about a minute, gave me a violent head ach" (24–25). Although the experience of the sublime from atop the bridge is overwhelming, one finds that by "descending then to the valley below, the sensation becomes delightful in the extreme. It is impossible for the emotions, arising from the sublime, to be felt beyond what they are here: so beautiful an arch, so elevated, so light, and springing as it were, up to heaven, the rapture of the Spectator is really indescribable!" (25). Again, the landscape is emblematic: Virginia's happiness could not be achieved without the intermediate stage of war, any more than Jefferson could avoid a violent headache when looking down from the bridge. Yet, seen from below, the bridge symbolizes pleasurable beauty on Virginia's horizon. A passage at the end of Query VI explicitly contrasts this horizon of promise with Great Britain's horizon of lost glory: "The sun of her glory is fast descending to the horizon. Her philosophy has crossed the Channel, her freedom the Atlantic, and herself seems passing to that awful dissolution, whose issue is not given human foresight to scan" (65).

The next five chapters shift from Natural to Civil History, focusing on the state's human resources. Jefferson begins with recently imported populations—settlers and slaves—then discusses the indigenous ones, reordering chronology to accentuate Native American society, which he depicts as the more harmonious of the two. In Query VIII, he argues against the "present desire of America . . . to produce rapid population by as great importations of foreigners as possible" (83). He proposes "natural propagation" instead, to avoid importation of the values of emigrants from absolute monarchies. His appeal is grounded in the principle of happiness defined as social harmony: "It is for the happiness of those united in society to harmonize as much as possible in matters which they must of necessity transact together. Civil government being the sole object of forming societies, its administration must be conducted by common consent" (84). One of the most invidious imported values, he argues, is acceptance of slavery, a practice that can only be an obstacle to social harmony. Query VIII ends on a note of hope stemming from the passage of a law prohibiting further slave importation. "This will in some measure," Jefferson writes, "stop the increase of this great political and moral evil, while the minds of our citizens may be ripening for a complete emancipation of human nature" (87).

The next two chapters, notably brief, respond to queries on the military and marine forces. Their brevity, it would seem, is in inverse proportion to their importance during the period in which *Notes* was first written—when Virginia, under Jefferson's governorship, was under siege by the British. Although *Notes'* "Advertisement" states that the "subjects are all treated imperfectly; some scarcely touched on," none is so sketchily drawn as these. Jefferson explains in the "Advertisement" that "to apologize for this [imperfect treatment of subjects] by developing the circumstances of the time and place of their composition, would be to open wounds which have already bled enough." But to include these queries at all contradicts this stated reticence to open old wounds. *Notes* was, after all, revised and published *after* America's victory. Thus, one reads the last sentence of Query X with the knowledge that it is no longer applicable: "Since the perfect possession of our rivers assumed by the enemy, I believe we are left with a single armed boat only" (91). The two queries seem to proclaim, rather than gloss over, how close Virginia came to defeat, thereby dramatizing Jefferson's narrative of maturation.

While Jefferson is bent on portraying Virginia as nature's chosen place, he is equally interested in establishing the newly independent nation as the world's place of choice. This is evident in Query XI, "Aborigines." Addressing the speculation that Native Americans were originally inhabitants of Asia who "passed into America" (100–101), Jefferson observes that a "greater number of . . . radical changes of language having taken place among the red men of America, proves them of greater antiquity than those of Asia" (102). Thus, according to this view, Native Americans are aboriginal not just to America but to the world. Jefferson mythologizes a Golden Age for America. In contrast to a theological Eden, however, which posits a lost age that won't be restored until God so wills, Jefferson's age of innocence is human-made and ongoing. Describing Native American societies as prior to the law, he cites their tribal groups as evidence of a moral sense and an aesthetic sensibility. Having "never submitted themselves to any laws, any coercive power, any shadow of government," he writes, their "only controuls are their *manners* and that *moral sense* of right and wrong, which, like the sense of tasting and feeling, in every man makes a part of his nature" (93; emphasis mine).

Jefferson's dichotomy between "savage Americans" who have "no law" and "civilized Europeans" who have "too much law" establishes the problematic of the law as a central theme of America's ethical aesthetics of liberty. If law is the Law of the Father, an abstract, noncontextualized imposition on the whole of society, formalizing historical inequalities, it is also the possibility of new laws that counteract and supplant the old. Comparing Native Americans and Europeans to sheep and wolves, Jefferson asserts that "the sheep are happier of themselves, than under care of the wolves" (93). However, instead of advocating no law for Virginia and America, *Notes* presents a case for republican law by contrasting the Native Americans' *law-less* morality with Great Britain's corrupt monarchical law.[8] The contrast reappears in Query XII's discussion of towns: there have been instances, Jefferson writes, when "the *laws* have said there shall be towns; but *Nature* has said there shall not, and they remain unworthy of enumeration" (109; emphasis his). With this, Jefferson ushers in the next category of queries, which, according to his Library Classification system, apply to Philosophy and Reason and prepare citizens to renounce monarchical law and support the laws of liberty.

Just as the foregoing queries (I–XII) portray Virginia as a growing child, those that treat Philosophy and Reason (XIII–XXII) depict the state as a young adult ready to take on the rights and responsibilities of ethical selfhood. Virginia as Body becomes the Body Politic, and the state's (and America's) capacity for self-governance becomes the crucial question. These queries propose a variety of practices by which individuals may stylize themselves as a way of becoming aesthetic-ethical citizens of liberty. Jefferson does not depict happiness in a subjunctive mood. For him it is attainable, through acts of self-stylization and societal formation. One reason these queries express such concern over the legacies of monarchical law, religious intolerance, slavery, and exploitive manufacturing is that they, too, are self- and society-forming practices, but not practices of virtue and harmony. Rather, they lead to the vices that Epicurean philosophy seeks to avoid: "desire and fear, the two principal diseases of the mind" (letter to William Short, Oct. 31, 1819).

Notes begins its critique of Virginia's inherited legal system by chronicling the state's constitutional history from colonial days, reiterating the grievances from the Declaration of Independence that left the colonies "no alternative . . . but resistance, or unconditional submission" (117). Jefferson devotes more than half of Query XIII to a discussion of the "very capital defects" in the newly framed state constitution, which, as the first one in America, was written by citizens in their own still-formative period, "when we were new and unexperienced in the science of government" (118). Arguing that the constitution concentrates too much power in the "same hands," which is "precisely the definition of despotic government" (120), Jefferson concludes with a plea for "the proper remedy; which is a convention to fix the constitution . . . to render unnecessary an appeal to the people, or in other words a rebellion, on every infraction of their rights, on the peril that their acquiescence shall be construed into an intention to surrender those rights" (129).

This concern to "fix the constitution" before rebellion becomes necessary contradicts Jefferson's oft-quoted remark to James Madison that "a little rebellion now and then is a good thing, and as necessary in the political world as storms in the physical" (letter to Madison, Jan. 30, 1787). But this contradiction is inevitable in the problematic between individual and state. Jefferson explains in his letter to Madison that he sees rebellion as inherent in republican forms of government. "The mass of mankind under [republican governments] enjoys a precious degree of liberty and happiness. It has its evils too: the principal of which is the turbulence to which it is subject. But weigh this against the oppressions of monarchy, and it becomes nothing." He goes on to point out, however, in terms that at least partially clarify his seeming denial in Query XIII of the value of rebellion, that "unsuccessful rebellions indeed generally establish the incroachments on the rights of the people which have produced them." He expresses hope that republican governors will be "so mild in their punishments of rebellions, as not to discourage them too much."

Thus, in this letter and in *Notes*, Jefferson can both defend the right of rebellion and argue that, given the risks of rebellion, it is imperative to establish "every essential right on a legal basis" (*Notes* 161). As subsequent chapters will show, this is a recurrent problematic in America's aesthetics of liberty. The effort to ensure social and political equality leads writers in this tradition to call for laws mandating equity but to oppose those that proscribe it. While it is consistent with the logic of an aesthetics of liberty to defend rebellion as a means to struggle against constraints on subjectivity, it is of equal or even greater importance to establish practices of ethical subjectivity that will diminish the need for rebellion; the writers under study here tend to view egalitarian law as such a practice and as worth preserving for that reason.

In Query XIV, entitled "Laws," the tension between the right of rebellion and respect for the law is starkly manifest, especially in the lengthy discussions of slave emancipation and public education. In those sections the tension is compounded by a prejudice against blacks and the poor. The first portion of Query XIV discusses Virginia's general retention of English common law. Jefferson points out the efforts then underway to revise the laws that retained the legacy of the monarchy, since they "inculcat[ed] principles inconsistent with republicanism" (137). Noting that 126 new acts had been proposed, he devotes the remaining two-thirds of the query to discussing and defending four of them: a plan for emancipating slaves, a proposal for proportioning punishments to crimes, a program for extending public education throughout the state, and lastly, in keeping with *Notes'* aesthetic orientation, a call for funding purchases of "books, paintings, and statues" to "begin a public library and gallery" (149). These four are given special attention because they are the most controversial, the least popular, and the most central to the realization of Jefferson's post-Revolutionary ethos.

Jefferson's discussion of the plan for emancipating "all slaves born after passing the act" reveals the tensions between equitable law and self-determination in *Notes'* aesthetics of liberty. He proposes that slaves

> should continue with their parents to a certain age, then be brought up, at the public expence, to tillage, arts or sciences, according to their geniusses, til the females should be eighteen, and the males twenty-one years of age, when they should be colonized to such places as the circumstances of the time should render most proper, sending them out with arms, implements of household and of the handicraft arts, seeds, pairs of the useful domestic animals, &c. to declare them a free and independant [*sic*] people, and extend to them our alliance and protection, till they shall have acquired strength. (137–38)

To replace the population lost in this recolonization, he further proposes that "an equal number of white inhabitants" be induced to migrate to America. This latter proposal goes against the grain of his earlier reservation about the importation of foreigners and is thus a gauge of the strength of his racial bias registered in this plan. Although *Notes* is remarkable in its time for its advocacy of slave emancipation, it is also a document of its time, a reflection of the Law of the White Father, which assumes the legal and social inferiority of blacks.[9]

The reader can see, in the arguments Jefferson uses to defend his emancipation plan, where *Notes* stands in relation to the hegemonic technology of power that legally sanctioned slavery. *Notes* asserts without reservation that blacks have no "depravity of the moral sense" (142). This adherence to Moral Sense over Lockean philosophy moves Jefferson's arguments toward a logic of equality and natural rights for all human beings. It is imperative on moral grounds, he argues, that the generation of blacks born after the passing of the law be freed and provided a means of independence. But what of the slaves born before the passing of the new law? In this case, it would appear, the Lockean principle of the right to "estate" for whites overrides rights of natural equality for slaves.

Jefferson's justification for exporting freed blacks is explicitly divided into political, physical, and moral arguments. He designates as political the "deep rooted prejudices entertained by the whites; ten thousand recollections, by the blacks, of the injuries they have sustained; new provocations; the real distinctions which nature has made; and many other circumstances" that will "divide us into parties, and produce convulsions which will probably never end but in the extermination of the one or the other race" (138). When it comes to rebellion of blacks against whites, then, rebellion is depicted as moving irrevocably toward extermination rather than possible resolution.

Jefferson's physical and moral arguments manifest a dread of resolution at least as much as a concern about perpetual "convulsions." "When freed," he states in closing, the slaves are "to be removed beyond the reach of mixture" (143). Several inconsistencies revolve around his idea of "mixture." An argument for miscegenation might logically have been made at this point, but the language of this passage represents mixture of black and white as abhorrent.[10] The ideal of harmony is used to support an aesthetics of racism, and "difference" is made the basis of black inferiority. Citing "the difference . . . fixed in nature" (138), Jefferson begins his argument by making skin color an issue. When referring to white skin, he celebrates mixture; when referring to black skin, he disdains it. "Are not the fine mixtures of red and white," he asks rhetorically, "the expressions of every passion by greater or less suffusions of colour in the one, preferable to that eternal monotony, which reigns in the countenances, that immovable veil of black which covers all the emotions of the other race?" (138). His aesthetics thus perpetuates white biases by advocating an opposition and hierarchical division in the name of "difference"; black skin is seen as monotonous rather than harmonious, and "flowing hair" and "a more elegant symmetry of form" are cited as marks of the "superior beauty" of whites. Difference is also said to reign in regard to mental faculties: "Comparing them by their faculties of memory, reason, and imagination, it appears to me, that in memory they are equal to whites; in reason much inferior, as I think one could scarcely be found capable of tracing and comprehending the investigations of Euclid; and that in imagination they·are dull, tasteless, and anomalous" (139). This ranking of mental faculties reiterates the movement of *Notes* from Memory to Reason to Imagination even as it shows how racism blinds Jefferson to the rationality, beauty, and artistry of blacks.

Jefferson's plan "to diffuse knowledge more generally through the mass of the people" (146) and his proposal for a public library and art gallery continue the metaphor depicting Virginia as a person maturing through the stages of Memory (History), Reason (Philosophy), and Imagination (the Fine Arts). Regarding the law for public education, he writes, "The general objects of this law are to provide an education adapted to the years, to the capacity, and the condition of every one, and directed to their freedom and happiness" (147). This plan, which attempts to formalize ethical practices for future citizens of Virginia, comprises three schools and three stages: "the schools of the hundreds, wherein the great mass of the people will receive their instruction" in history; grammar school for languages, which is "chiefly a work of memory"; and the university, where students may "study those sciences which may be adapted to their views" (147–48).

Jefferson challenges the mainstream religious model of education by arguing that "instead . . . of putting the Bible and Testament into the hand of the children, at an age when their judgments are not sufficiently matured for religious enquiries, their memories may here be stored with the most useful facts from Grecian, Roman, European and American history" (147). And, attempting to reconcile collective and individual morality, he points out that "the first elements of morality too may be instilled into their minds; such as, when further developed as their judgments advance in strength, may teach them how to work out their own greatest happiness, by shewing them that it does not depend on the condition of life in which chance has placed them, but is always the result of a good conscience, good health, occupation, and freedom in all just pursuits" (147). Following the developmental line of thought, Jefferson argues that languages are appropriate to the "period of life, say from eight to fifteen or sixteen years of age, when the mind, like the body, is not yet firm enough for laborious and close operations" (147). The university then takes up the next stage of development, when the individual is better prepared to deal with Anatomy and Medicine, Natural Philosophy and Mathematics, Moral Philosophy, the Law of Nature and Nations, the Fine Arts, and Modern Languages (curriculum outlined in Query XV, 150). Jefferson defends the plan for public education as a means of extending suffrage, thus "rendering the people the safe, as they are the ultimate, guardians of their own liberty" (148). Query XIV closes with a proposal to extend public education by establishing a public library and gallery.

These formulations for public education are notably democratic for their time, but they are also implicated in the normalizing mechanisms of emerging bio-power. Part of their normalizing function is the continuation of gender and class divisions that were inscribed within America's educational system from the outset. Girls are not considered to be part of the plan at all. And the elitist skimming system creates a triangle whose broad base includes all, regardless of intellectual merit and class, but whose narrow apex admits only "twenty of the best geniusses" from the working class. Jefferson's discussion of the

poor incorporates metaphors of rigid class division. He proposes, for example, that the brightest of the poor children who
are to be instructed at public expense be "raked from the rubbish" (146). Thus, while his notion of genius or "natural aristocracy" opposes a self-perpetuating aristocracy based on wealth,
it also accepts the hierarchical assumptions endemic to bourgeois society.

All of the texts treated later in this study grapple with the
problematic of extending education without extending its disciplinary powers. Reading Jefferson's proposals for public education in the context of emerging forces of bio-power helps us
discern the ways in which formalizations of a pedagogy fostering
self-stylization can comply with or convert into a pedagogy of
normalization. This is an ongoing and inevitable problem for any
ethics espousing an aesthetics of liberty, a problem that requires
continual vigilance and struggle to democratize education.

Queries XV through XXII continue the focus on issues crucial
to the development of the new social order inaugurated by the
Revolution. They address ways to fight corruption while Virginia and America are still in a formative period. In particular, "Religion," "Manners," and "Manufactures" follow the classical Greek idea that ethical selfhood and virtuous citizenry
are formed through exercises that train the mind and body. In
Query XVII, "Religion," for example, Jefferson depicts the activities of "reason and free enquiry, [as] the only effectual agents
against error" (159). The "present state of our laws on the subject of religion," he argues, is one of "religious slavery" (158,
159). In contrast to Query XIV's use of difference as a reason to
avoid mixing whites and blacks, this argument presents differences of thought as a healthy corrective to a coercive "uniformity
of opinion," insisting that "reason and persuasion are the only
practicable instruments" for spreading religion (160). He supports his appeal for religious tolerance with Epicurean logic: the
disharmony that might occur from having many different sects in
contest with one another is slight compared to the "convulsion"
that inevitably will occur if religious rights are not granted. Employing a feminine metaphor to indicate freedom (consonant

with his notion of beauty as feminine), he cites the "sister states of Pennsylvania and New York" as evidence that even the possibility of slight disharmony is diminished when religious freedom is guaranteed, for in these states where religious tolerance is assured, "harmony is unparalleled" (160–61).

"Manners" argues that slavery, like religious intolerance, is a training ground for vice. "The whole commerce between master and slave," Jefferson states, "is a perpetual exercise of the most boisterous passions, the most unremitting despotism on the one part, and degrading submissions on the other" (162). His pleas for emancipation "with the consent of the masters, rather than by their extirpation" (163) are pleas for an alternative ethos for both master and slave, as outlined in Query XIV's plan for emancipation, education, and recolonization.

"Manufactures" describes agrarian labor as an *askesis* intended to cultivate virtue in American citizens and their land. Arguing from a stance of utility derived from Epicureanism and affirmed in Moral Sense philosophy, Jefferson points out that a "difference of circumstance . . . should often produce a difference of result" within various societies. Thus Europe's land-scarce economy provides no useful model for America's "immensity of land," which, he suggests, suits "the industry of the husbandman" (164). The argument for pursuing agrarian practices for as long "as we have land to labour" follows the principles of an aesthetics of liberty in which the individual is responsible for improving self and society. "Is it best," Jefferson inquires rhetorically, "that all our citizens should be employed in its improvement, or that one half should be called off from that to exercise manufactures and handicraft arts for the others?" (164). What distinguishes the land-laborer from the manufacturer, he explains, is the dependence of the latter on the "caprice of customers," for "dependence begets subservience and venality" (165). Those "who labour in the earth" cultivate a virtue of subsistence that strengthens the land, their own bodies, and the republic, whereas the "mobs of great cities add just so much to the support of pure government, as sores do to the strength of the human body." Furthermore, "it is the manners and spirit of a people which preserve a republic in vigour. A degeneracy in these is a canker which soon eats to the heart of its laws and constitution" (165).

These metaphors of vigor and degeneracy of body reflect the concern over good health that runs throughout *Notes*. For example, Jefferson's descriptions of sublimity culminate in a headache, and his explanation for not dwelling on the war is that to do so might "open wounds which have already bled enough." This concern with health is understandable as a personal response to his wife's illness and death and to his own injury and convalescence. But such concern is also characteristic of an aesthetic ethics in which beauty and vigor of mind and body are esteemed and are used as a model of well-being for the social body. What is perhaps most important to note is that during this period in which medicine emerged as an apparatus of bio-power, Jefferson advocated care of the self instead of medicalization of the self. He was profoundly critical of hospitals, castigating the "general hospital, where the sick, the dying, and the dead are crammed together, in the same rooms, and often in the same beds." Jefferson held that "Nature and kind nursing [by friends and neighbors] save a much greater proportion in our plain way, at a smaller expence, and with less abuse" (134).

Query XX concludes the section of *Notes* devoted to Virginia's present (young-adult) stage of development. There Jefferson speculates on the near future when America, cleared of the debts of its war of independence, might "come to measure force hereafter with any European power" (174). He strongly urges his readers to avoid war: "Young as we are, and with such a country before us to fill with people and with happiness, we should point in that direction the whole generative force of nature, wasting none of it in efforts of mutual destruction. It should be our endeavor to cultivate the peace and friendship of every nation, even of that which has injured us most, when we shall have carried our point against her" (174). Instead of gaining more territory or fishing rights, Americans should expend money only "in improving what they already possess, in making roads, opening rivers, building ports, improving the arts, and finding employment for their idle poor." These practices would "render them much stronger, much wealthier and happier. This I hope will be our wisdom" (174–75).

The twenty-third and final chapter of *Notes* turns to the subject of writings about Virginia and thus concludes the book with a focus on the fine arts. As was noted earlier, *Notes* depicts America as still "a child of yesterday," though developing and showing signs of greater artistry. In Jefferson's ethics, the fine arts evolve from practices of aesthetic citizenship; thus, the writing of *Notes* is itself an *askesis* for his personal development. At the beginning of the chapter he criticizes the styles of previous historians, noting that Captain Smith, though "honest, sensible, and well informed," possessed a "barbarous and uncouth" style and that the reverend William Stith, though a "man of classical learning, and very exact," had "no taste in style" and was "inelegant" (177). It may be presumed that Jefferson tried to be more elegant; yet, in keeping with his hope for continuing aesthetic and ethical maturation for himself and America, he concludes his work by noting its limitations. In this vein, he bids his readers to "accept [*Notes*] as the result of my labours, and as closing the tedious detail which you have so undesignedly drawn upon yourself" (179).

This final chapter carries out the earlier developmental logic: with a chronological study of American state papers, it recapitulates the story of Virginia from its physical founding to the 1776 Declaration of Independence—from dependent colony to interdependent state. Since declaring itself independent, Jefferson points out, "this state has had no controversy with any other, except with that of Pennsylvania, on their common boundary," and the result of that was a "happy accommodation of their rights" (178). *Notes* thus concludes with an assertion of current happiness that bodes well for the continued pursuit of happiness by the citizens of Virginia and America.

If the pursuit of happiness, which the Declaration of Independence asserts is an inalienable right, has proven more difficult than *Notes*, at times, implies it would be, this is because the right of pursuit has not been granted equally to all. Jefferson acknowledges as much in "Manners," where he makes certain of his doubts explicit: "Indeed I tremble for my country when I reflect that God is just: that his justice cannot sleep for ever: that considering numbers, nature and natural means only, a revolution of the wheel of fortune, an exchange of situation, is among possible events: that it may become probable by supernatural interference! The Almighty has no attribute which can take side with us in such a contest" (163). This rare reference to the possibility of divine intervention in human affairs bespeaks the otherwise suppressed realization that, as long as America remained a slave nation, any future efforts for a "happy accommodation" of rights between slave and free states would prove impossible.

Jefferson died on July 4th, 1826, the fiftieth anniversary of the Declaration of Independence. Three years later, his worst fears regarding insurrection by blacks were confirmed by the publication of David Walker's *Appeal*. In the *Appeal*, the black American voice that Jefferson's works silence is heard full-force. The complete title indicates Walker's intended audience: "To the CO-LOURED CITIZENS OF THE WORLD, but in particular, and very expressly, to those of THE UNITED STATES OF AMERICA." The repetition of the phrase "Our Wretchedness" in the title of each of the *Appeal*'s four articles rings out in mockery of the emptiness of the claims of liberty and pursuit of happiness that the Declaration of Independence avows as every man's right. Walker's text, in short, is the American slaves' declaration of independence. In the final pages, excerpts from the Declaration are juxtaposed with demands that whites "compare your own language . . . with your cruelties and murders inflicted by your cruel and unmerciful fathers and yourselves on our fathers and on us—men who have never given your fathers or you the least provocation!!!!!!" (75). As a call to arms of all blacks, enslaved or freed, this is a crucial text in the American ethical tradition of an aesthetics of liberty.

The *Appeal* is also an explicit response to Jefferson's *Notes*. It is important, Walker states (in keeping with an ethics of self-stylization), that "blacks *themselves*" refute Jefferson. In the preamble, Walker states his reason for writing to blacks rather than appealing to the conscience of white Americans or resting content with the refutations of white abolitionists. He explains that he seeks "to awaken in the breasts of my afflicted, degraded, and slumbering brethren, a spirit of inquiry and investigation respecting our miseries and wretchedness in the *Republican Land of Liberty!!!!!!*" (2). That spirit of inquiry leads him to problematize Jefferson's concept of happiness, for as Walker indicates, slaveowners are "happy to keep in ignorance and degradation, and to receive the homage and labour of the slaves" (3). But it is not happiness that Walker opposes. Rather, he shows that happiness ultimately will be impossible not only for slaves but for slaveowners, because slavery will lead inevitably to insurrection.

In the first of his four articles, entitled "Our Wretchedness in Consequence of Slavery," Walker explicitly confronts Jefferson's assertions in Query XIV that blacks are inferior to whites in appearance and mental capacity. Regarding skin color, he counters the aesthetic bias of whites: "They think because they hold us in their infernal chains of slavery, that we wish to be white, or of their color—but they are dreadfully deceived—we wish to be just as it pleased our Creator to have made us" (12). About interracial marriage, he observes that, as far as he is concerned, "I would not give a *pinch of snuff* to be married to any white person I ever saw in all the days of my life" (9). Turning to the issue of mental capacity, he urges blacks to obtain copies of *Notes* and refute Jefferson's charges in order to demonstrate to whites their error in judgment. He points out that "there are some talents and learning among the coloured people of this country, which we have not a chance to develope, in consequence of oppression," implying that once freedom and equal education are accorded blacks, these talents will flourish (14–15).

The remaining three articles in the *Appeal* address more extensively the issues of education, religion, and recolonization of blacks. Article II argues the importance of literacy for the practice of freedom. As Walker states, "[F]or coloured people to acquire learning in this country, makes tyrants quake and tremble

on their sandy foundation" (31). Here and in the following article, he indicates the ways in which reading and writing become
weapons against an oppression that is reinforced in racist texts
and in the educational and religious institutions of America.
Then, in Article IV, he focuses on the issue of recolonization of
slaves, discussing in particular Henry Clay's proposals for a colony in Africa. Walker's opposition to this plan is adamant. "Let
no man of us budge one step," he advises, for "America is more
our country, than it is the whites—we have enriched it with our
blood and tears" (65).

Walker's call to arms against slavery appropriates for his people the Declaration's combative rhetoric of freedom. And his advocacy of education as a means to fight oppression promotes the
freedom of the black subject. The *Appeal* concludes with the
threat that caused Jefferson to tremble: that God will not be on
the side of the slaveowners. "The Americans may be as vigilant
as they please," Walker warns, "but they cannot be vigilant
enough for the Lord, neither can they hide themselves, where he
will not find and bring them out" (76). Just as *Notes* and the
Declaration founded the discourse of America's aesthetics of liberty, David Walker's *Appeal* founded an aesthetics of liberty for
blacks, using the same principles of equality and beauty to fire
the slaves' struggle for liberty.

CHAPTER TWO

The Reproduction of Liberty: Becoming Fuller's *Woman in the Nineteenth Century*

Margaret Fuller was an uncommon woman in the Age of the Common Man. Indeed, through her writings and Conversations, she challenged a number of that era's most widely accepted definitions of democratic progress and freedom. In her articles for the *Dial* and the New York *Tribune* and in her two full-length works, *Summer on the Lakes* (1844) and *Woman in the Nineteeth Century* (1845), Fuller demonstrated how the prevailing conceptions of masculinity and femininity reinforced a subordination of women that would necessarily prevent America from attaining democracy. She did so by drawing on principles of self- and civic-artistry integral to an American ethics of an aesthetics of liberty. Like *Notes on the State of Virginia*, *Woman in the Nineteenth Century* portrayed human beings individually and collectively as *homo aestheticus*. But Fuller challenged Jefferson's aesthetics of liberty with her call for full rights and responsibilities of citizenship for women. Although in *Notes* Jefferson asserted equality between men and women, his concept of the rights of citizenship applied exclusively to free men. For him, women's happiness and ethical development were to be attained in the domestic sphere. *Woman in the Nineteenth Century* disrupted this masculinist view by arguing that an American aesthetics of liberty without women's full citizenship was neither aesthetic nor ethical.

In the preface to *Woman*, Fuller characterizes the work as an extended version of her essay "The Great Lawsuit—Man *versus* Men; Woman *versus* Women." That title, she explains, was meant "to intimate the fact that, while it is the destiny of Man, in the course of the ages, to ascertain and fulfil the law of his being, so that his life shall be seen, as a whole, to be that of an angel or messenger, the action of prejudices and passions which attend, in the day, the growth of the individual, is continually obstructing the holy work that is to make the earth a part of heaven." She goes on to explain that, by "Man," she means "both man and woman; these are two halves of one thought" (13). True to this account of the original article, *Woman* attempts the double task of presenting evidence for progress toward the fulfillment of human destiny while critiquing current social practices. As Fuller puts it, women must "ascertain what is for them the liberty of law"—their proper destiny—and must not uncritically accept a mere "extension of partial privileges" (14).

In this chapter, I will discuss that double task as it is manifest in the form of *Woman,* in its concept of gender aesthetics, and in its construction of female subjectivity as a process of becoming Woman. These are all means by which Fuller problematizes several primary technologies of power—the law, the family, sexuality, and education—that intersect to form masculinity and femininity within white, bourgeois culture. Although Fuller, like Jefferson, argues for emancipation of the slaves, her ethics focuses most profoundly on white, bourgeois culture and power formations. Her problemization of Jefferson's notion of virtue for women does not extend to a rethinking of race differences but, rather, subsumes black women within the category of white women. This is not to say that Fuller was indifferent to the oppression of black women; in *Woman* she expressly condemns their enslavement. But her most significant and sustained arguments embrace all women, precisely as women, in resisting new forms of normalizing power.

The particular emphasis Fuller gives to law, marriage, schooling, and sexuality may be understood as a response to changing conditions of power in the eighteenth and nineteenth centuries. As Foucault points out in the first volume of *History of Sexuality,* during this period one longstanding technology of patriarchal power—the deployment of alliance—was subsumed in (without being supplanted by) another patriarchal technology—the deployment of sexuality. Both are normalizing systems, but they operate through different mechanisms. The deployment of alliance that predominated in the West prior to the eighteenth century was "a system of marriage, of fixation and development of kinship ties, of transmission of names and possessions." It operated through "mechanisms of constraint," especially law (106). Gradually, the deployment of sexuality was superimposed on the system of alliance. This technology functioned not through legal constraint but by "proliferating, innovating, annexing, creating, and penetrating bodies in an increasingly detailed way, and in controlling populations in an increasingly comprehensive way" (107).

The deployment of sexuality, Foucault argues, took shape from practices of alliance, particularly from the religious practices of confession and penance. In the deployment of sexuality, these practices expanded into the domains of medicine, education, police surveillance, and psychiatry. For example, a primary operation in the deployment of sexuality was the "hysterization of women, which involved a thorough medicalization of their bodies and their sex . . . carried out in the name of the responsibility they owed to the health of their children, the solidity of the family institution, and the safeguarding of society" (146–47). The bourgeois family became the "interchange of sexuality and alliance" (108), with the mother at the nexus of this interchange. She could be the Good Mother who carried out her responsibility to the social body by procreating and properly educating her children. Or she could be a negative version of the Mother, either the sexual but nonprocreative woman or the procreative but "nervous woman" (104). Within the power formation of the family, all women were daughters whose *telos* was married motherhood; those who did not marry were obligated to remain celibate and to perform functions of societal motherhood.

Feminist historians have dealt extensively with the cultural symbols that were integral to the superimposition of sexuality onto alliance. As Laurel Thatcher Ulrich has shown, early eighteenth-century ministerial discourse in America portrayed motherhood with deep ambivalence, defining women through the symbolism of both Eve and Mary. Benjamin Wadsworth, for example, gravitated toward the idea that every woman was Eve, writing in 1712 that "persons are more apt to *despise a mother* (the weaker vessel, and frequently more indulgent) than a father." John Flavell concurred, charging that a mother, "by reason of her blandishments, and fond indulgence is most subject to the irreverence and contempt of children." Yet during this same period, Ulrich notes, Thomas Foxcroft and Cotton Mather treated motherhood as being especially worthy of respect, Mather going so far as to compare the love of a mother with the love of God (71–75). Toward the end of the eighteenth century, popular works like Rousseau's *Emile* cast a new light on common presumptions about women's simultaneous inferiority and superiority to men. Although Rousseau declared that "woman is made [by nature's law] to submit to man and to endure injustice at his hands," he added that her role in the "physical and moral order" compensated for her natural inferiority (Book V: 359, 321). He argued that, because each woman was endowed with a morality that enabled her to curb her own excesses of passion as well as her "master's," men were actually "dependent on the weaker" sex (Book V: 323).

Rousseau's gender-based master-slave dialectic helped empower what Barbara Welter has called the Cult of True Womanhood, which achieved ideological dominance in the nineteenth century. The "four cardinal virtues" of True Womanhood—"piety, purity, submissiveness and domesticity"—valorized physical chastity for single women; a sexually active, unmarried woman was a " 'fallen angel' " whose deserved fate was either "madness or death" (152–54). Married women were expected to remain pure through sexual submissiveness to their husbands and domestic service to their families. Thus, the Eve-Mary conjunction of puritan discourse became sentimentalized in the Cult of True Womanhood. Such sentimentality, which linked the bearing of children both to Eve's sorrow and to Mary's holiness, arose from the interpenetration of the technologies of alliance and sexuality.

This sentimentality was often promoted by women themselves as they became writers and teachers during the late eighteenth and early nineteenth centuries. Nina Baym and Jane Tompkins have argued persuasively that sentimentality in women's fiction is a form of resistance to an ethics based on masculinist authority that valorizes rationality and devalorizes compassion. Yet, when we examine such works in the context of the power networks of alliance and sexuality, we see the limits of this form of resistance. The nineteenth-century educator and writer Catharine Beecher (*A Treatise on Domestic Economy*) exemplified these limits. In keeping with the law of alliance, Beecher insisted that women were subordinate to men by divine decree. Furthermore, her advocacy of improved education for women on the basis of their higher morality helped restrict women to a prescriptive morality, which, on behalf of the social body, they were to pass on to their children. "Let the women of a country be made virtuous and intelligent," Beecher advised, "and the men will certainly be the same" (13). The education that Beecher proposed and offered in her own schools was meant to ready women for their God-given mission to "renovate degraded men" (13). In constructing a concept of womanhood and motherhood according to which women were to serve as America's moral messiahs, Beecher and her sister Harriet Beecher Stowe, among others, further embedded women in the familial nexus of alliance and sexuality.[1]

This new investment of power appears in a number of equally notable works that focus on the "pathologies" of bourgeois family life. In Hawthorne's *The Marble Faun*, as well as in psychiatric and police campaigns, incest became increasingly textualized as part of the process that Foucault described as the putting of sexuality into discourse. The growing concern to ensure "normal" sexuality within the bourgeois family bears witness to the extent to which sexuality was problematized in the nineteeth century. Although the men and women who upheld women's moral superiority challenged masculinist authority, they did so in a way that perpetuated women's subordination to men both individually, within the family, and collectively, in governance. They complied with and even fostered the almost exclusively male authority of the emerging medical science and law that were beginning to supplant masculinist religious authority.

Fuller's feminist theorizing took place within this cultural context. Although she, like Jefferson, embraced assumptions about human perfectibility that were inherently teleological, her work dramatically disrupted the normalizing technologies of power operating in her historical period. Indeed, the idea of human perfectibility was itself a challenge to the Calvinist notion of a fallen humanity born into sin. What is of particular interest here is the way in which Fuller developed the idea of women's perfectibility. *Woman*'s innovations in form, its challenges to accepted notions about gender, its assaults on established law and labor practices, and its promotion of a new form of subjectivity for women resisted the systems of alliance *and* sexuality. *Woman* advocated ethical responsibility for women without being entrapped by essentializing arguments about women's moral superiority. It forwarded new forms of community and pleasure through an aesthetics of liberty in which men and women were equal partners in the artistry of self and society.

*I*n her journal, in words of rather harsh self-judgment, Fuller records her interest in creating a new form of writing. "For all the tides of life that flow within me," she writes, "I am dumb and ineffectual, when it comes to casting my thought into a form. No old one suits me. If I could invent one, it seems to me the pleasure of creation would make it possible for me to write" (quoted in Chevigny 63). Fuller's search for a new way to express thought comes to fruition in *Woman*.[2] And that experiment in form may also be seen as an experiment in self-formation. She employs a dialogic form that is more complex than either the query-response format of Jefferson's *Notes* or the dialogues in her own *Summer on the Lakes*. In *Woman,* Fuller explicitly uses dialogue to textualize ideas she opposes, juxtaposing the writings of others with her own, thereby presenting conversation as a mode of and model for individual and species development. *Woman's* nonhierarchical, conversational form disrupts the normalizing discourses of the dominant social order and provides a model for their reformulation.

As Mikhail Bakhtin has argued, the use of dialogue, most often associated with the novel, decenters and deprivileges an authorial voice and approaches more closely than a monologic style the heteroglossia of language. Fuller uses dialogue to challenge not only Romanticism's valorization of the autonomous voice of artistic genius but also the religious and secular authority of patriarchal prose that claims for itself the exclusive power to assign meaning. The first words of the text exemplify the way her conversational mode is geared to disrupt fixed meaning. She begins with two well-known quotations: "Frailty, thy name is Woman" and "The Earth waits for her Queen." She then offers the following comment: "The connection between these quotations may not be obvious, but it is strict. Yet would any contradict us, if we made them applicable to the other side, and began also,

> Frailty, thy name is Man.
> The Earth waits for its King?" (15)

Responding to her own question, she indicates that she accepts both versions of these axioms; both Man and Woman are frail and yet full of promise.

Through such reaccentuation of dichotomous characterizations of women, Fuller inserts into nineteenth-century discourse on the Woman Question a key but missing term: the Man Question. What will men have to do in order for women to attain the perfection of Womanhood? In *Woman,* the answer to this question is, "Let [women] think; let them act; till they know what they need. We only ask of men to remove arbitrary barriers"

(172). Such barriers are clearly obstacles to women's ethical self-transformation. But Fuller also insists that when men erect arbitrary barriers for women, they simultaneously undermine their own freedom. Men and women, she suggests, must be dialogically engaged in the stylization of freedom.

In one of *Woman*'s most novelistic dialogues, a feminist voice confronts the voice of a masculinist slave trader. Though it is lengthy, I quote the passage in its entirety to indicate the extent to which the dialogue is spoken as if by characters in a novel:

"Is it not enough," cries the irritated trader, "that you have done all you could to break up the national union, and thus destroy the prosperity of our country, but now you must be trying to break up family union, to take my wife away from the cradle and the kitchen-hearth to vote at polls, and preach from a pulpit? Of course, if she does such things, she cannot attend to those of her own sphere. She is happy enough as she is. She has more leisure than I have,—every means of improvement, every indulgence."

"Have you asked her whether she was satisfied with these *indulgences?*"

"No, but I know she is. She is too amiable to desire what would make me unhappy, and too judicious to wish to step beyond the sphere of her sex. I will never consent to have our peace disturbed by any such discussions."

" 'Consent—you?' it is not consent from you that is in question—it is assent from your wife."

"Am I not head of my house?"

"You are not the head of your wife. God has given her a mind of her own."

"I am the head, and she the heart."

"God grant you play true to one another, then! I suppose I am to be grateful you did not say she was only the hand. If the head represses no natural pulse of the heart, there can be no question as to your giving your consent. Both will be of one accord, and there needs but to present any question to get a full and true answer. There is no need of precaution, of indulgence, nor consent. But our doubt is whether the heart *does* consent with the head, or obeys its decrees with a passiveness that precludes the exercise of its natural powers, or a repugnance that turns sweet qualities to bitter, or a doubt that lays waste the fair concessions of life. It is to ascertain the truth that we propose some liberating measures." (28–30)

Although this exchange gives the feminist the final word, there is no finality to her words. Instead, Fuller's feminist expresses doubt about male rationality—the rule of the "head"—as well as about male superiority.

Another long passage of dialogue expresses the feminist views of "Miranda," whose life history bears a recognizable resemblance to Fuller's. Miranda adopts the Emersonian value of self-reliance and reaccentuates it within a non-Emersonian context of women's rights, arguing that women's self-reliance is impeded by "guardians, who think nothing is so much to be dreaded for a woman as originality of thought or character" (40–41). To the extent that Miranda is an alter ego of Fuller, this passage may be seen as a form of self-scrutiny that enables her to confront herself through writing: an important process in an ethical aesthetics of liberty. To the extent that Miranda represents Fuller's ideal of Virgin-Motherhood, which I will discuss below, she signifies an ethical femininity necessary to developing Womanhood. Miranda challenges traditional definitions of masculinity and femininity that treat certain forms of virtue—and virtuosity—as innate features of masculinity. Hence her concluding words: "Let it not be said, whenever there is energy or creative genius, 'She has a masculine mind' " (43).

Beyond its inclusion of dialogue, *Woman* is dialogic in drawing on the discourses of mythology, literature, religion, science, and the arts. This intertextuality—which has sometimes been denigrated by critics as digressive—enacts a collectivity consonant with the work's stated convictions. A notable example is the discussion of the present "crisis in the life of woman," in which Fuller presents overviews and analyses of three male "prophets of the coming age"—Swedenborg, Fourier, and Goethe—lauding them for their "noble" views of women. Although she charges that Swedenborg's writings contain "arbitrary and seemingly groundless" derogatory views on women, she commends him for allowing "room for aesthetic culture and the free expression of energy" that would foster women's growth as well as men's (123). Arguing that Fourier and Goethe advocate transformations that can be only partial, the former looking to institutions alone and the latter to individuals, she uses each to intervene against the assumptions of the other. To Fourier she gives the Goethean advice that if attempts to reform society "are made by unready men, they will fail" (125). And to Goethe, with his exclusive emphasis on self-culture, she offers Fourier's argument that "bad institutions are prison walls and impure air that make [a man] stupid, so that he does not will" (124–25). In other words, Fuller promotes artistry of *both* self and society, insisting that each fosters the other.[3]

A centripetal principle of organization operates over and against the centrifugal forces of conversation or dialogue in *Woman*. Fuller draws on Proclus's philosophy of the four spheres to provide a unifying model of development for her aesthetic ethics, even as she employs dialogical thinking to disrupt the hierarchical tendencies of any teleological vision. As she explains:

> Proclus teaches that every life has, in its sphere, a totality or wholeness of the animating powers of the other spheres; having only, as its own characteristic, a predominance of some one power. Thus Jupiter comprises, within himself, the other twelve powers, which stand thus: The first triad is *demiurgic or fabricative,* that is, Jupiter, Neptune, Vulcan; the second *defensive,* Vesta, Minerva, Mars; the third, *vivific,* Ceres, Juno, Diana; and the fourth, Mercury, Venus, Apollo, *elevating and harmonic.* In the sphere of Jupiter, energy is predominant—with Venus, beauty; but each comprehends and apprehends all the others. (118)

Using this teaching as a guide for individual development, Fuller proposes that all animate being has the potential to develop through stages corresponding to the spheres. "The law of

right, the law of growth . . . speaks in us, and demands the perfection of each being in its kind—apple as apple, Woman as
Woman" (177). With the energies of the first sphere, associated
with childhood, one can develop toward the fourth sphere, associated with adulthood and beauty. Like Jefferson before her and
Thoreau after, Fuller employs tropes of life stages to portray a
process of development that can be stunted at any moment. And
like them, she draws on an aesthetics that depicts the energies of
the sublime—of Jupiter's "Titanic childhood"—as a means of
moving toward the beautiful—maturity as represented by Venus.

Fuller applies an ideal of aesthetic development not only to
individuals but to history, depicting humanity's development in
terms of the four spheres. She argues that, once humanity has
"subjugated its brute elements," then "criticism will have per-
ished; arbitrary limits and ignorant censure be impossible; all
will have entered upon the liberty of law, and the harmony of
common growth" (118). That is, when individual people reach
the fourth sphere, where "community of life and consciousness
of mind begin among men," then human development will have
attained the beauty of liberty, a liberty unconstrained by the limits of old laws and practices (118). But no such growth is possible, Fuller warns, until women are given the same opportunities
that [white] men have. In the words of her oft-quoted dictum:
"We would have every arbitrary barrier thrown down. We
would have every path laid open to Woman as freely as to Man"
(37).

The passage from Proclus also provides rhetorical coherence
for *Woman,* which has no conventional structuring devices such
as chapter divisions. The work's argument unfolds describing a
Golden Age followed by the four stages of humanity that correspond to Proclus's four spheres: the fabricative, the defensive, the
vivific, and the harmonic. In the Golden Age, the "All-Creating
wandered on the earth to taste, in a limited nature, the sweetness
of virtue" (18). (Whether Fuller accepted such an era as actual
prehistory is irrelevant, as we can see from her later note on a
different subject. About the claim of the daughter of Linnaeus to

have witnessed a "spirit" hovering above a red lily, she concedes, "It is true, this, like many fair spirit-stories, may be explained away as an optical illusion, but its poetic beauty and meaning would, even then, make it valuable, as an illustration of the spiritual fact" [117].) In *Woman,* the Golden Age represents an ideal toward which humankind should aspire. "These were the triumphant moments; but soon the lower nature took its turn, and the era of a truly human life was postponed" (18).

The next stage of Fuller's argument (19–43) contrasts the Golden Age with the beginnings of human history, which Fuller associates with Proclus's first sphere. During this era, the energies of Jupiter, Neptune, and Vulcan predominated. Men made themselves masters of women, and white men committed brutalities against Native Americans and blacks (25). In this section, Fuller catalogues the myriad ways in which men have enslaved women: by treating them as property in marriage, taking ownership of their children, denying them education, denigrating them in religious imagery, subjecting them to physical violence, and so on. Despite these injustices, she claims that, "no doubt, a new manifestation is at hand, a new hour in the day of Man" (20).

In the next section (43–93), Fuller justifies her hope for "a new hour" in human history. She cites the countless examples of men and women, in legend and in history, who have challenged the injustices of men's rule. These challengers represent Proclus's defensive sphere, associated with Vesta, Minerva, and Mars. Fuller points out that in the ancient world, where women were held to be inferior, the "idea of Woman" was nonetheless noble and brave: "Even Victory wore a female form" (55). Exemplary women closer to Fuller's time were Elizabeth I, Isabella, and the Polish revolutionary Emily Plater. She identifies their willingness to battle for freedom as evidence that in the "present crisis" the "preference is given to Minerva" (118). Finally, Fuller notes the progress already evident in the marriage laws of some countries and argues that, if women were completely free, their exchange in the deployment of alliance would no longer hold: "[A woman] would not, in some countries, be given away by her father" (71). Neither would coercive pressures (of the deployment of sexuality) require a woman to marry: "Nor, in societies where her choice is left free, would she be perverted, by the current of opinion that seizes her, into the belief that she must marry, if it be only to find a protector, and a home of her own" (71).

Fuller turns next to possibilities for change, evoking Proclus's vivific sphere (93–168). As outlined in *Woman,* this sphere corresponds to a "New Era" in which social institutions undergo significant transformation. More than half of *Woman* is devoted to discussion of how this stage might come about and what would constitute it. Among the hopeful signs of change, Fuller cites the "triumphs of Female Authorship" (93), improvements in education for girls (94–95), and the growing numbers of unmarried women and female spiritual and moral leaders (96–115). In this section, she introduces her notion of gender aesthetics and discusses Proclus's account of the three goddesses of the third sphere: Ceres, goddess of grain; Juno, queen of Jupiter; and Diana, protectress of the hunt and of women. As symbols of fertility, marriage, and virginity, respectively, they suggest for Fuller the coming of a historical period in which women's new strength and leadership will emerge.

The final section of *Woman* recapitulates the whole of Fuller's argument (168–79). Evoking Proclus's "elevating and harmonic" fourth sphere as a description of humanity's potential, Fuller links ethical development and beauty. However, this potential human destiny with its new kind of woman is depicted more as expectation than as actuality. Using the course of a day as a metaphor for human development, Fuller locates herself "in the sunny noon of life. Objects no longer glitter in the dews of the morning, neither are yet softened by the shadows of evening. Every spot is seen, every chasm revealed" (178). From such a position of partial development, she argues, one is able to "read" the traces of history, to comprehend the broken "effigies that once stood for symbols of human destiny" (178), and to discern possibilities for aesthetic growth. And doing so is to learn to "cherish your best hopes as a faith, and abide by them in action"(178).

*F*uller once observed, in a *Daily Tribune* review of Emerson's essays, that although history could rightfully "inscribe his name as a father of the country, for he is one who pleads her cause against herself," his writings were "sometimes obstructed or chilled by the critical intellect." She further commented that he had "raised himself too early to the perpendicular and did not lie along the ground long enough to hear the secret whispers of our parent life," adding that she wished that "he might be thrown by conflicts on the lap of mother earth, to see if he would not rise again with added powers" ("Emerson's Essays" 393–94). Her wish to warm Emerson's chilled intellect— expressed somewhat ambivalently in this inverted allusion to Samson's loss of power at Delilah's lap—is a key to the theory of gender that Fuller develops in *Woman.* Her view of human development involves a gender aesthetics that challenges the essentialist concepts—integral to the technologies of alliance and sexuality—according to which masculinity is equated with maleness and femininity with femaleness. For, as Fuller states, "it is no more the order of nature that [femininity] should be incarnated pure in any form, than that the masculine energy should exist unmingled with it in any form" (115). What ails Emerson's chilled intellect, she implies, could be treated with a dose of the "feminine" which "flushes, in blossom, the face of the earth, and pervades, like air and water, all this seeming solid globe, daily renewing and purifying its life" (115).

As Lois Magner has pointed out, Fuller employed the scientific idioms of her day to advance feminist principles, using metaphors of electricity and magnetism, for example, to disrupt notions of fixed gender. Drawing on such metaphors, she undermined the notion that "male and female represent the two sides of the great radical dualism": rather, "they are perpetually passing into one another. Fluid hardens to solid, solid rushes to fluid. There is no wholly masculine man, no purely feminine woman" (115–16). Fuller argued further, against the notion of fixed binary sexual difference, that both history and nature provide ample evidence that there is no one-to-one correspondence between masculinity and men and femininity and women:

> History jeers at the attempts of physiologists to bind great original laws by the forms which flow from them. They make a rule; they say from observations what can and cannot be. In vain! Nature provides exceptions to every rule. She sends women to battle, and sets Hercules spinning; she enables women to bear immense burdens, cold, and frost; she enables the man, who feels maternal love, to nourish his infant like a mother. Of late she plays still gayer pranks. . . . Presently she will make a female Newton, and a male Syren. (116)

On the basis of nature's gay pranks, Fuller defends "free play" for all marginalized people. Such freedom is necessary, she argues, so as not to impede "creative energy": that energy will "take what form it will, and let us not bind it by the past to man or woman, black or white" (117). Fuller's arguments thus proceed from the premise that diversity is natural, while efforts to contain and curb multiplicity are not: hence her repeated demands that humanity "be wise, and not impede the soul" (117).

Fuller's concluding summary of her theory of gender aesthetics is itself a playful parody of orthodox ecclesiastical rhetoric. As she puts it, she will "retrace, once more, the scope of my design in points, as was done in old-fashioned sermons" (168). Her design—a retelling of the creation and fall—is, by traditional American religious standards, blasphemous. According to Fuller's "sermon" and in keeping with Proclus's notion of the four spheres, the teleology of Man is beauty and harmony, but this aesthetic-ethical objective requires schooling on earth until all of humanity is "perfectly happy or virtuous" (169). Ideally, the growth of Man is two-fold, masculine and feminine"; it proceeds by "two methods," which may be distinguished as "Energy and Harmony; Power and Beauty; Intellect and Love" (169). These two sides of human development could be expressed in Man and Woman in "perfect harmony," so that "they would correspond to and fulfill one another, like hemispheres, or the tenor and bass in music" (170).

It is important to consider Fuller's gender aesthetics within the framework of her era as well as ours. From the perspective of contemporary radical feminist analysis, Fuller's categories are implicated in essentialism insofar as masculinity is defined as energy, power, and intellect, and femininity as harmony, beauty, and love. Yet her gender categories were not biologically determined. Her concept of androgyny dislodged assumptions about women's reproductive capacities and physical inferiority that were normative in her time. Furthermore, Fuller's gender aesthetics remain relevant for contemporary feminism in three important ways. First, her theorizing does not erase differences; rather, she accentuates diversity and ongoing transformation. Second, she eschews the liberal feminist notion that women should become more like men. "Were they free, were they wise fully to develop the strength and beauty of Woman," she argues, "they would never wish to be men, or man-like" (63). Third, she does not advocate androgyny as a means to human liberation but, rather, argues for women's political, social, and economic equality as a means to social harmony.[4]

Fuller's explanation for humanity's lack of harmony underscores this point. The reason is precisely that men have held women in servitude. As she tells it:

> Man in the order of time, was developed first; as energy comes before harmony; power before beauty.
>
> Woman was therefore under his care as an elder. He might have been her guardian and teacher.
>
> But, as human nature goes not straight forward, but by excessive action and then reaction in an undulated course, he misunderstood and abused his advantages, and became her temporal master instead of her spiritual sire.
>
> On himself came the punishment. He educated Woman more as a servant than a daughter, and found himself a King without a Queen. (170).

Woman's version of the Book of Genesis thus contains no serpent, no apple, no Eve as first sinner; and it requires no sacrificial death to redeem a fallen humanity. Fuller lays the burden of blame for humanity's thwarted development squarely on the shoulders of men. She argues further that men's subordination of women resulted in women's relatively less corrupted moral development: "For, as too much adversity is better for the moral nature than too much prosperity, Woman, in this respect, dwindled less than Man, though in other respects still a child in leading-strings" (171). Gradually, because of women's more developed (but not essentially different) morality, "men became a little wiser." Over the course of history, "no age was left entirely without a witness of the equality of the sexes in function, duty and hope" (172). Such witnesses, both men and women, are antetypes of the new era of humanity.

In place of salvation after death through Christ, Fuller foretells the birth of a new race of humanity on earth. She envisions the coming of a "woman who shall vindicate their birthright for all women; who shall teach them what to claim, and how to use what they obtain" (177). At an earlier point in the text, Fuller calls this woman the "Virgin-Mother of the new race" (102); later, reiterating the term, she asserts: "Would she but assume her inheritance, Mary would not be the only virgin mother" (177).[5] Pondering whether the name of such a woman shall be "for her era Victoria, for her country and life Virginia," Fuller decides that "predictions are rash," for "she herself must teach us to give her the fitting name" (177). In accordance with the book's gender aesthetics and dialogical ethics, the new Woman will not be an Adamic namer of others but, rather, will teach humanity how to converse.

Although it is idle to speculate whether Fuller believed herself to be this new woman, I am not the first to think she did. Such proclamations as "I must beat my own pulse true in the heart of the world; for *that* is virtue, excellence, health" (178) sounded an imperious tone that drew dramatically polarized responses from her contemporaries. Sophia Hawthorne, for example, responded to "The Great Lawsuit" with outright derision, inquiring in a letter to her mother what she thought "of the speech Queen Margaret has made from the throne," and observing that it seemed to her "that if she were married truly, she would no longer be puzzled about the rights of woman" (quoted in Chevigny 231). Ednah Dow Cheney, on the other hand, wrote that "it was this consciousness of the illimitable ego, the divinity in the soul, which was so real to Margaret herself, and [was] what she meant in her great saying 'I accept the universe,' which gave her that air of regal superiority which was misinterpreted as conceit" (quoted in Chevigny 230). Thus, both Hawthorne and Cheney associate Fuller with the regality that she attributes to the new "Queen."

More to the point than whether Fuller regarded herself as Virgin-Mother and Queen of the new race is the way she used such terms to advance her ethics, widening the horizons of meaning within language. *Woman* reinvests some of the most patriarchally marked of English words with feminist meanings. By appropriating the religious symbolism of the Christian Madonna, the mythological symbolism of virgin goddesses, and the royal symbolism of queenhood, Fuller both defuses the patriarchal power invested in those concepts and redefines the terms whereby one achieves Womanhood. The threat to the patriarchal order posed by the idea of queenship for all women is illustrated in Nathaniel Hawthorne's *Blithedale Romance*. In the carnival scene, as Dale Bauer points out, Zenobia, by "enacting the fantasy of her Queenship, . . . introduces not simply a reversal of roles, but a breakdown in the hierarchy between masculine and feminine. She brings ambivalence into this world, disorder into Coverdale's order of things" (38).

It is by the light of these new meanings, Fuller proposes, that "innocence is to be replaced by virtue, dependence by a willing submission, in the heart of the Virgin-Mother of the new race"

(102). The new women will not be bound by the conventional language through which religious and secular laws and norms prescribe the conditions of their sexuality and reproduction. They will ascertain that the "liberty of law" requires laws of liberty and will submit to the law of liberty alone. Fuller reproves American laws and practices that create barriers to women's development. In *Woman,* the struggle against such laws and practices is a training ground for aesthetic-ethical womanhood. Fuller's redefinitions of maternity, virginity, and queenliness forcefully question masculinist prescriptions regarding women's political, familial, sexual, spiritual, and reproductive activities. By problematizing the language of the laws and customs that subject women to the rule of men and by recording instances of resistance throughout history, *Woman* promotes a freer subjectivity for all American women.

For example, in her exploration of the familial nexus of masculinist laws and women's reproduction, Fuller addresses the contentions of men that "Woman seems destined by nature . . . for the the inner circle" (34). She points out that if this were indeed the case, then "the arrangements of civilized life have not been, as yet, such as to secure it to her. Her circle, if the duller, is not the quieter. If kept from 'excitement,' she is not from drudgery" (34). Fuller goes on to deride the hypocrisy of the ostensible protectors of women by pointing out that those "who think the physical circumstances of Woman would make a part in the affairs of national government unsuitable, are by no means those who think it impossible for negresses to endure field-work, even during pregnancy, or for sempstresses to go through their killing labors" (35).

Masculinist, racist civilization, she argues, justifies its subordination of all women as necessary for "protective" purposes. This is particularly the case when female reproductive capacities are used to restrict women's liberty and marriage laws are used to ensure women's subordination. At the same time, many women—slaves and the working poor—are forced to perform labor that endangers their health. Fuller explains how the laws of her time subjugate women, excluding them from certain occupations, preventing them from owning property, allowing "idle" and "profligate" men to rob working wives of their wages, and legally sanctioning only a father's custody of children. It "may well be an Anti-Slavery party that pleads for Woman," Fuller observes (31). Through this evocation of the abolitionist cause, she indicates the interconnections between the forms of power that enslave black women and those that normalize all women into servility.

Seeking to eliminate the form of marriage in which women suffer legal, social, and economic subordination, Fuller describes four types of equal marriages already to be found: household partnership, mutual idolatry, intellectual companionship, and religious union (72–82).[6] Although she argues that each of the first three types, even mutual idolatry, is superior to the hegemonic form in which wives are subordinate to husbands, she advocates the fourth as most desirable. She applauds the religious union because, as a "pilgrimage towards a common shrine," it includes the "home sympathies," "household wisdom," and "intellectual communion" of the others while also striving toward the improvement of humanity (80–81). This form of union requires profoundly ethical men and women, whom she calls "Los Exaltados, Las Exaltadas," for "from them would issue a virtue by which [the world] would, at last, be exalted too" (155). Describing "a youth and a maiden" she knows as "both aspiring, without rashness, both thoughtful, both capable of deep affection, both of strong nature and sweet feelings, both capable of large mental development," she hails them as the "harbingers and leaders of a new era," for their minds are "truly virgin, without narrowness or ignorance" (155).

Given the prevailing definition of a virgin as a person (usually female) who has not had sexual intercourse, Fuller's appropriation of the term to describe virtue regardless of sexual experience or gender is as heretical as her appropriation of the right to deliver "old-fashioned sermons." Through the reaccentuation of the concept of virginity, *Woman* problematizes Victorian notions of sexuality in several ways. Regarding the double standard that prescribes chastity for unmarried women yet allows or sanctions sexual experience for unmarried men, Fuller points out the consequence that "a great part of women look upon men as a kind of wild beasts" (150–51) (a judgment that might well exacerbate the sexual incompatibility between men and the women who adhere to Victorian standards of True Womanhood). She notes, further, that many women are beginning to doubt the possibility of their own virtue as long as they are in danger of corruption from men ruled by their own passions; women wonder "whether virtue is not possible, perhaps necessary, to Man as well as to Woman" (148). And, finally, Fuller uses the idea of a "virgin mind" to defend women like Mary Wollstonecraft and George Sand against the denunciations they endured because of their sexual practices. Seeking to supplant superficial judgments about sexual chastity with a concern for spiritual purity, she pays tribute to these women, so "rich in genius, of most tender sympathies, capable of high virtue and a chastened harmony, [who] ought not to find themselves, by birth, in a place so narrow, that, in breaking bonds, they become outlaws" (75).

Fuller also defends women who do not carry out the obligation to marry and procreate. In reply to the derision heaped on unmarried women, whose number increased in the nineteenth century (and among whom she may have counted herself at the time of writing), Fuller asserts boldly: "We shall not decline celibacy as the great fact of the time" (119). She argues that women who are "undistracted by other relationships" may well gain "a closer communion with the one" (97) and makes celibacy of mind and spirit a vocation for all women, whether they form attachments to men or not. "I would have Woman lay aside all thought, such as she habitually cherishes, of being taught and led by men," she writes. And, advising women to turn from male sons toward the Sun of Truth, she puns: "I would have her, like the Indian girl, dedicate herself to the Sun, the Sun of Truth, and go nowhere if his beams did not make clear the path" (119).

Fuller sees power in this kind of self-reliance whereby women can promote causes beyond their own independence. Her call for women to join the abolitionist cause (118–19) clarifies her earlier claim that the "power of continence must establish the legitimacy of freedom." Fuller enjoins women to say to men involved in slavery that "if they have not purity, have not mercy, they are no longer fathers, lovers, husbands, sons of yours" (167). Furthermore, to oppose slavery must be part of women's ethical self-stylization: just as men must stop constructing obstacles to women's freedom, so, too, women must help eliminate the barriers to freedom for American slaves.

The form of aesthetic–ethical subjectivity for women that Fuller proposes in *Woman* combines a "virgin mind" with "maternal wisdom."[7] These virtues are to be attained by a series of practices through which a woman might become Woman: a form of subjectivity that reflects the principles of equality and diversity. Fuller documents the ways women have sought and struggled for the freedom of the subject. Cataloguing the many women warriors of legend and history, she shows that fighting for freedom is a crucial practice of self-formation. She especially esteems women who joined in military battle, like Joan of Arc and Emily Plater, "the heroine of the last revolution in Poland" (45). And women authors, educators, and community leaders earn her special notice for reaching beyond domesticity into the civic sphere. Thus, *Woman* avoids prescribing the practices women should undertake but, rather, seeks to open as many avenues as possible, avenues that would let women become whatever they might, whether sea captains, carpenters, or senators (174) . "As preparatory to the senate," Fuller states in a passage about readying men and women for civic responsibility, "I should like to see a society of novices, such as the world has never yet seen, bound by no oath, wearing no badge" (154). *Woman in the Nineteenth Century* may be read as a handbook for a society of aesthetic–ethical novices.

Fuller's work as writer, educator, and Conversationalist places her alongside Jefferson as an exemplar of and a major contributor to America's ethical aesthetics of liberty. *Woman*'s interventions against the constraining powers of the deployment of alliance and the enticing powers of the deployment of sexuality were rewarded in 1848, three years after its publication. That year, at Seneca Falls, New York, members of the women's and abolitionist movements formalized the demand for women's rights by drafting and signing the *Declaration of Sentiments*. That same year, having completed a unique training in the practice of freedom by writing *Woman*, Margaret Fuller became a revolutionary in the Italian struggle for independence.

CHAPTER THREE

The Care of the Chaste Self: Thoreau's *Walden* and the Desexualization of Masculinity

*W*hat is chastity? How shall a man know if he is chaste?" ponders Thoreau in "Higher Laws" (220). And then the silent thunder of his judgment: "He shall not know it" (220). If we take this declaration by itself, we will perhaps be forced to conclude that Thoreau has failed in the mission he announces in the opening pages of *Walden* and, despite himself, has written "an ode to dejection." But the note of defeat in this passage is offset by those preceding and following it, for "Higher Laws" also suggests that a man can and should strive to *become* chaste despite not knowing whether he *is* chaste. And about the desirability of men's acquiring chastity, Thoreau expresses no doubt: "Chastity is the flowering of man; and what are called Genius, Heroism, Holiness, and the like are but various fruits which succeed it" (219–20). Furthermore, he does not hesitate to fix upon a means for becoming chaste: "If you would be chaste, you must be temperate," he advises, and adds without reservation that "from exertion come wisdom and purity; from sloth ignorance and sensuality" (220).

Toward the end of "Higher Laws," Thoreau turns to more specific means whereby one might become chaste. He debunks John Farmer's mistaken practice of "some new austerity" by which Farmer tried merely to "let his mind descend into his body and redeem it"; Thoreau then addresses the question how one's body might, instead, "actually migrate thither" (222). To describe this ethical migration, he uses aesthetic imagery, saying, "Every man is the builder of a temple, called his body, to the god he worships, after a style purely his own, nor can he get off by hammering marble instead" (221). He continues this description of self-artistry by observing that "we are all sculptors and painters, and our material is our own flesh and blood and bones. Any nobleness begins at once to refine a man's features, any meanness or sensuality to imbrute them" (221)

This passage brings to light the basic concerns of Thoreau's ethical aesthetics of liberty: concerns about the body, the intellect, and the imagination in acts of self-stylization. Thoreau held that chastity was not the exclusive domain of women and that it was neither an obligation to confess sexual impurity nor an act of sexual self-denial but, rather, a practice of liberty grounded in techniques of self-transformation. This view profoundly challenged dominant discourses about purity, sexuality, and masculinity. It opposed the "separate-sphere" ideology of antebellum America, with its dichotomous ideals of a private, nuclear family inspired by feminine morality and an autonomous, success-oriented business world led by masculine prowess, which was gradually formalized during the course of the nineteenth century through the normalizing operations of the deployment of sexuality.[1]

Walden's treatment of chastity sheds light on this crucial formation of power/knowledge, which emerged in nineteenth-century America, especially as it affected white, middle-class men. In *Notes*, Jefferson expressed more interest in the body politic and the body of Virginia than in the individual body. Despite his concerns about health, he discussed bodies primarily in criticizing the deployment of alliance's powers of death, torture, and confinement as punishment for certain crimes (*Notes* 144–45). But *Notes*' advocacy of new laws and pedagogy also promoted the disciplinary functions of those domains of power that operated through the body. By Fuller's and Thoreau's time, the proliferating power networks of the deployment of sexuality had begun to supplant the power formations of the deployment of alliance. This shift from alliance to sexuality was not uniform for women and men or in all social institutions. As I have argued in chapter 2, women remained subject to the laws and constraints of alliance even as they were increasingly subjected to the genera tive power mechanisms of the deployment of sexuality. Fuller responded to these interlocking power relations by resisting both the legal prescriptions of the deployment of alliance and the newer social constraints of the deployment of sexuality.

Walden, too, registers the shifting yet interlocking relations of alliance and sexuality, but focuses more on practices and values directly affecting the lives of American men. Like Fuller, Thoreau deals with issues of law and bodily constraint associated with the deployment of alliance. His call to overturn the slavery laws, for example, is a response to the regime of alliance. But, for the most part, *Walden* is directed against an enslavement to customs of diet, domesticity, commerce, work, clothing, and education: practices of a different order. These practices function by incorporating "normality" through bodily self-surveillance and self-regulation. Within the American bourgeois family, sons are regulated into the Norm of the Father, whose domain is traversed by the power mechanisms of Oedipal desire and industrial capitalism. This nexus of power technologies of alliance and sexuality dictates that the son's economy of pleasure must derive from marriage to a woman, a surrogate mother, over whom he will exercise control to ensure his paternity. The familial field of power is crossed over by that of capitalist production, which develops the son into a family wage-earner.

The treatment of such issues in *Walden* shows how the shift from alliance to sexuality involved a new construction of masculinity and how Thoreau challenged that construction. That is, as a particularized narrative of a white, well-educated, middle-class American man—rather than as the universalized account of human experience that it is often taken to be—*Walden* questions the practices and values of its time in regard to how men are normalized. This is not to say that *Walden* proposes an ethics for men only—it certainly includes women—but its most profound challenges address the restricted individual freedom characteristic of normalized masculinity.

The deployment of sexuality operates on the male subject through psychiatric, eugenic, and economic mechanisms sanc-

tioning the "normality" of heterosexuality, of familial procre-
ation, and of exclusive wage-earning responsibility. Men are thus
objectified in three ways: their pleasures are heterosexualized,
their fertility is medicalized, and their labor is capitalistically
economized. Within the technology of sexuality, these prescriptions of normality and perversity are understood as defining
one's core identity (*History of Sexuality* 43). In opposition to the
prescription of a masculine identity defined in terms of normalized (hetero)sexuality, Thoreau proposes the care of the self as a
practice of chastity—a chastity not defined in sexualized terms.
In place of the quest for certainty that pervades the deployment
of sexuality and its "hermeneutics of desire," the care of the self
proposes a set of exercises for acquiring the truth of chaste existence rather than confirming the pre-existent truth of one's "inner" being. Writing is one of those exercises, and as such, *Walden*
is itself a form of *askesis*, an exercise of reflecting on these exercises in chaste subjectivity.

In indicating what it means to become chaste, *Walden* follows
the traditional etymology of the word *chastity* defined as purity
of body, mind, and art. Derived from the Latin *castitas, castita-
tis* under the influence of the adjective *castus*, which means
"morally pure, chaste, holy," the related adjective "chaste" also
designates an "artistic or literary style" that is "without meretri-
cious ornament." In *Walden*, the making of one's life into an aesthetic text is a quintessential practice of chastity. And by
indicating that chastity—as an ongoing art of existence—exceeds
human knowing, Thoreau places it in a domain of infinite meanings that resist the will to know characteristic of the deployment
of sexuality.

The importance of infinite meanings in Thoreau's aesthetic
ethics is underscored by his assertion that "if we knew all the
laws of Nature, we should need only one fact, or the description
of one actual phenomenon, to infer all the particular results at
that point" (290).[2] But "we know only a few laws" and are
therefore like mountain travelers: while the mountain has "absolutely but one form," we confront an "infinite number of

profiles" (290–91). And this is "no less true in ethics" (291). Rather than despairing over infinite interpretability, Thoreau proposes that each person become a reader and writer of multiple meanings. Denouncing as "brain-rot" the view that "in this part of the world it is considered a ground for complaint if a man's writings admit of more than one interpretation," he argues that the "words which express our faith and piety are not definite; yet they are significant and fragrant like frankincense to superior natures" (325). This embrace of infinite interpretability is integral to *Walden*'s depiction of an aesthetics of liberty that requires the care of the self through exercises in chastity. But it is important to recall that for Thoreau the mountain, ultimately, has "one form." His aesthetic ethics incorporates the dual assumption of one form with an infinite number of profiles.

Thoreau begins his account of chaste selfhood with an enigmatic disclosure: "I long ago lost a hound, a bay horse, and a turtle-dove, and am still on their trail" (17). His story of following their "trail" illuminates the paradox that one may become chaste even if one cannot abstractly know that one is chaste.[3] Each of the figures represents a way of knowing and a form of experience or, combining the two, a technique of selfhood. Thoreau names three cognitive modes, linking the hound with the senses, the horse with the intellect, and the dove with the imagination. His three forms of experience—states of individual and species development—are hunting, technology, and artistry, which he links to the hound, horse, and dove, respectively. The search for the lost creatures entails learning to live by the ways of knowing and experiencing that each represents. Because Thoreau attaches a multiplicity of meanings to the three figures, this learning involves practices that can lead one to become either more imbruted or more chaste. Thus, he depicts a complex process whereby one draws on unchanneled, instinctual energy—the "generative energy" of the wild—in order to "migrate thither," that is, refine oneself as a work of art.

The discursive threads Thoreau spins around the figures of the hound, the bay horse, and the turtledove create a pattern very much like a web: a configuration befitting the notion of one form with many profiles. Like the hound, horse, and dove, spiders and their webs are used in *Walden* to suggest both the obstacles to and the possibilities of a chaste life. Of *Walden*'s six references to spiders, the first two present a web as something that ensnares. Discussing the hazards of being "harnessed" to material goods like furniture, Thoreau observes that one's "gay butterfly is entangled in a spider's web then" (66). And in "Sounds," he describes the seemingly regulated chant of the whippoorwills as an insistent buzzing all around him, "like a fly in a spider's web, only proportionately louder" (124).

We find, however, that spiders and webs, like mountains, may be variously interpreted. Furthermore, the interpretations depend on one's state of purity. Thoreau's subsequent interpretations of webs reflect his chaste conduct. Increasingly, he identifies himself with spiders. In "Solitude," he dispels the notion that being alone makes him lonely: "I am no more lonely," he insists, than "the first spider in a new house" (137). In "Housewarming," he shares his "dream of a larger and more populous house, standing in a golden age"—a house with various places people might occupy, perhaps even "aloft on the rafters with the spiders" (243). The ice that forms over Walden Pond with its twice-frozen holes brings this observation: "When such holes freeze, and a rain succeeds, and finally a new freezing forms a fresh smooth ice all over, it is beautifully mottled internally by dark figures, shaped somewhat like a spider's web" (293). Appearing in conjunction with Thoreau's own transformations, the spider web comes to signify beauty. And in the "Conclusion," with further enhancement of his aesthetic capacities, the self-spider identification becomes explicit: "If I were confined to a corner of a garret all my days, like a spider, the world would be just as large to me while I had my thoughts about me" (328).

To "borrow a trope" from Thoreau (in the spirit of his advice that a scholar might "borrow a trope" from the "savages" because they "have dwelt near enough to Nature and Truth"), becoming chaste is like spinning a spider's web. It is not a linear or hierarchical process of leaving behind each stage in order to reach a higher one. Instead, all strands of knowledge and experience are equally vital, all meeting or supporting the others; strength increases with greater intricacy of design. The more intricate the web of chastity, the greater the number of meanings through which one describes oneself and the world. Such an ethics acknowledges that a multiplicity of meanings prohibits certainty and power over the Not-Me by the Me; and it supplants the will to power with a refusal to be determined and regulated by the power/knowledge formations that separate the Me from the Not-Me. Because Thoreau's ethics resist the normalizing practices of American manhood, its approach to personal freedom and civic responsibility has potential to affect the lives of men and women alike. It is in this sense that *Walden* may be read as a "movement of desexualisation" seeking "new forms of community, co-existence, pleasure" (Foucault, "The Confession of the Flesh" 220).

I am the hounded slave," proclaims Whitman in "Song of Myself." In *Walden*, Thoreau similarly fuses the identities of the pursued and the pursuer, threading together references to hounds, nature, and humanity to represent the most basic and potentially base features of human existence. Throughout, the hound signifies the power of the senses, a power that at times assures the hound's survival but at other times entraps it in its own instincts. Human beings, likewise, are potentially both beneficiaries and victims of their senses. Thoreau proposes an ethics whereby one learns to measure one's senses in the creation of a selfhood that accentuates both personal freedom and chastity. In *Walden*'s references to dogs in general and hounds in particular, we can see how the senses aid or hinder the search for knowledge and chaste experience according to Thoreau's aesthetics of liberty.

Walden's early passages on dogs expound the dangers of sensuous indulgence, which leads not to satisfaction but to a life of "quiet desperation." After his "I long ago lost" disclosure, Thoreau next mentions a dog while discussing clothes in "Economy." Pointing out the foolishness of accepting outward garb as the measure of a person's ethics, he recounts the story of "a dog that barked at every stranger who approached his master's premises with clothes on, but was easily quieted by a naked thief." Thoreau imputes a similar tendency to human beings, most of whom confuse character with ornament and thus are robbed of self-value (22).

The next three references to dogs associate them with humankind's tendency to kennel itself. It is all too easy, Thoreau warns, to find oneself "in a workhouse, a labyrinth without a clew, a museum, an almshouse, a prison, or a splendid mausoleum" (28). Citing as an alternative to these places of surveillance the large wooden boxes he has spotted by the railroad, he puns that, by using one for a night's shelter, one could at least avoid "any landlord or house-lord dogging you for rent" (29). Then, perhaps with some exaggeration, he admits that he nearly purchased the Hollowell farm and inventories the attractions of the place, specifying its isolation as the greatest. Here, he recalls a time when he passed an isolated house on the river, aware of its location behind a grove of red maples only because in passing he "heard the house-dog bark" (83). Because the purchase did not go through, Thoreau writes, he avoided getting his fingers "burned by actual possession" (82). Finally, in another reference linking dogs, superficial knowledge, and entrapment in a power network of surveillance, Thoreau catalogues the news coverage he could do without: among the irrelevancies, "one mad dog killed" (94).

In *Walden's* next discussion of canine creatures, they represent an anachronistic, unstylized, and hence unchaste mode of cognition and experience. In "Sounds," Thoreau describes hearing the rumble of a cattle train with a "carload of drovers . . . in the

midst, on a level with their droves now, their vocation gone, but
still clinging to their useless sticks as their badge of office" (122).
Associating these drovers—these now driven herders—with
their herding animals, he asks, "But their dogs, where are they?"
and then comments on the herd dogs' growing uselessness:

> It is a stampede to them; they are quite thrown out; they have lost
> the scent. Methinks I hear them barking behind the Peterboro'
> Hills, or panting up the western slope of the Green Mountains.
> They will not be in at the death. Their vocation, too, is gone.
> Their fidelity and sagacity are below par now. They will slink
> back to their kennels in disgrace, or perchance run wild and strike
> a league with the wolf and the fox. So is your pastoral life whirled
> past and away. (122)

Though a trace of regret for the disappearance of the pastoral
life surfaces here, Thoreau displaces any nostalgia with his later
declaration that, in contrast to an animal, the human being "goes
a step or two beyond instinct, and saves a little time for the
fine arts." It is clear which vocation he regards as more timely
(253–54).

Again, in a discussion in "Visitors" of the French-Canadian
woodchopper, Thoreau focuses on the necessity to get beyond
instinct as the only technique for knowing and experiencing oneself and the world. Although Thoreau evinces a friendly attitude
toward what he considers Therien's primitivism, he nonetheless
points out its limitations. The woodchopper's closest companion
is his dog, with which he lives and travels and to which he is
frequently indebted for a dinner of freshly caught woodchuck.
Thoreau describes the woodchopper as having been "cast in the
coarsest mould" into a "stout but sluggish body." His body is
"gracefully carried," however, and his "dull sleepy blue eyes,"
are occasionally "lit up with expression" (145). Furthermore,
Thoreau represents Therien's woodchopping as a productive interaction with nature: in contrast to the mercenaries who have
"browsed off all the wood on Walden shore" (192), Therien cuts
his trees to ensure that "the sprouts which [come] up afterward

might be more vigorous" (146). So skillful is his woodchopping that Thoreau calls it "his art."

Nevertheless, after bestowing ample praise on the woodchopper, Thoreau clearly states what he views as limitations on his friend's capacity to act freely. "In him the animal man chiefly was developed," he remarks. And although this quality could be manifested pleasantly enough in "an exuberance of animal spirits," for the most part, the woodchopper's animality hindered his aesthetic-ethical development. The "intellectual and what is called the spiritual man in him were slumbering as in an infant," (147) and no amount of maneuvering "could get him to take the spiritual view of things; the highest that he appeared to conceive of was a simple expediency, such as you might expect an animal to appreciate; and this, practically, is true of most men" (150).

Although Thoreau stresses the importance of becoming more than a mere "animal man," he does not reject the instinctual. The next passage alluding to a hound shows how the very animality that encourages simple expediency is also necessary for survival under certain circumstances—and is more useful than "plantation manners." Remarking that runaway slaves sometimes stopped at this place on their way north, he notes that they "listened from time to time, like the fox in the fable, as if they heard the hounds a-baying on their track" (152). Here the hound, used by slaveowners to hunt their human prey, symbolizes the system of slavery. Furthermore, this passage predicts the breakdown of that system to the extent that the runaways can use their foxlike senses to escape the hounds on their trail.[4]

As Thoreau links the woodchopper, the slaveowner, the runaway, and the majority of human beings to the hound because of their animality, so, in "Higher Laws," he links the hound with himself. He reports a surging-up of an animal impulse within him: an urge to hunt and feed upon animal flesh. Returning home through the woods at dark after fishing, he recalls, "I caught a glimpse of a woodchuck stealing across my path, and felt a strange thrill of savage delight, and was strongly tempted to seize and devour him raw; not that I was hungry then, except for that wildness which he represented" (210). If on that occasion Thoreau only felt and reflected on his temptation, later, he readily enacted his desire: "Once or twice, . . . I found myself ranging the woods, like a half-starved hound, with a strange abandonment, seeking some kind of venison which I might devour, and no morsel could have been too savage for me" (210). This was the occasion for his controversial avowal: "I love the wild not less than the good" (210).[5]

Thoreau's homage to the wild as well as the good provides a key to his aesthetics of liberty and chastity. Like Jefferson and Fuller, but guided by his own concerns, Thoreau employs an aesthetic of the sublime and the beautiful to describe the process whereby one becomes an artist of the self. In *Walden*, the good—distinct from but not opposed to the wild—is synonymous with the refined and the beautiful. The wild, on the other hand, is a form of the sublime, an instinctual energy manifest sensually in eating, drinking, copulating, and so on, intellectually as the unfathomable, and imaginatively as an interrogation of truth. The good depends on the wild for its very existence; that is, it can arise only from what Thoreau calls the "generative energy" of the wild. He translates these aesthetic categories into experiential ones by correlating the wild with hunting and the beautiful with artistry, arguing that individuals and the species have the potential (eventually) to evolve from a hunting stage to an aesthetic one.[6]

However, Thoreau represents a qualified optimism about the potential for individual evolution within a given lifetime. In "Higher Laws," he writes that the young man "goes thither at first as a hunter and fisher, until at last, *if he has the seeds of a better life in him*, he distinguishes his proper objects, as a poet or naturalist it may be, and leaves the gun and the fish-pole behind" (213; emphasis mine). This view may be located within the general domain of discourse on evolution that emerged in the mid-nineteenth century. *Walden* contains one reference to Darwin, but Thoreau's notions about human evolution seem to be more in keeping with Herbert Spencer's interpretations of Darwin than with Darwinism as it is now understood. Thoreau's view of savagery as unevolved human primitivism reflects the hierarchy of the "civilized" over the "savage" that was becoming formalized in the human sciences of his period. The beginnings of this formalized hierarchy were evident in the eighteenth century's romanticized notion of the "noble savage."

Thoreau romanticizes, somewhat, the primitive practices that will be discarded when the species evolves. Recalling that boyhood hunting provided his own "closest acquaintance with Nature," he asserts that there "is a period in the history of the individual, as of the race, when the hunters are the 'best men,' as the Algonquins called them" (212). He points out, further, that hunting encourages empathy with nature, for "no humane being, past the thoughtless age of boyhood, will wantonly murder any creature, which holds its life by the same tenure that he does. The hare in its extremity cries like a child" (212). Thus, boys who hunt learn of the precariousness of life when (and if) they perceive themselves as both hunter and hunted.

According to this evolutionary ethical model, then, hound-like conduct will be discontinued by those who mature. But Thoreau cites the example of a "hunting parson" to suggest that continuing practices of primitivism can arrest maturation. "Such a one might make a good shepherd's dog," he conjectures wryly, "but is far from being the Good Shepherd" (213), for the practice of goodness, expressly identified with aesthetic existence, entails eating fruits and vegetables rather than animals. The "gross feeder is a man in the larva state; and there are whole nations in that condition, nations *without fancy or imagination*, whose vast abdomens betray them" (215; emphasis mine). Thoreau's personal admission of meat eating thus confirms that he, like the species as a whole, remains somewhere between the wild and the good. But despite his own practices, he has "no doubt that it is a part of the destiny of the human race, in its gradual improvement, to leave off eating animals, as surely as the savage tribes have left off eating each other when they came in contact with the more civilized" (216).

Although Thoreau's views of the primitive and the civilized partake of the hierarchies of nineteenth-century anthropology, he rejects the dichotomy between primitive and civilized sense experience. According to this dichotomy—a secularized version of innate depravity versus divine grace—the wildness or animality within must be totally suppressed for the sake of civilization. But Thoreau does not propose to cut off the forces of sensuality that nurture the hunter stage, with which the figure of the hound is linked. Instead, he sketches a gradual process of evolution that draws from the sensual, the primitive, and the wild and refines them into the pure, the good, and the chaste. Thus, for Thoreau, the wild is not to be negated. It is to be re-articulated. This view bears some resemblance to Freud's concept of sublimation (the similarity derives from their use of the discourses of organicism and developmentalism, which, as Foucault has shown, constituted the invention of Man); however, Freud's concept is best characterized as a hermeneutics of desire, not an aesthetics of existence. Thoreau does not frame his conceptualization in a vocabulary of sexuality, according to which libidinal desire is transformed into artistic creativity. Nor does he see the wild as a function of the psyche alone. Rather, the wild as well as the good are practices that constitute selfhood.

In Thoreau's conceptualization of this process, the good requires the wild, for it is the "generative energy [of the wild] which, when we are loose, dissipates and makes us unclean, [and] when we are continent invigorates and inspires us" (219). And in opposition to normalized discourses, which simultaneously suppress but obsessively elaborate through displacement what Bakhtin calls the "lower bodily stratum," Thoreau holds that no act in and of itself resides outside the domain of purity. He praises the Hindoo lawgiver who "teaches how to eat, drink, cohabit, void excrement and urine, and the like, elevating what is mean" (221). According to "Higher Laws," the care of the chaste self is a process not of rejecting the body in favor of a metaphysical state but, rather, of embodying purification: of elevating the mean. However, Thoreau projects humanity's elevation of the mean into the future. Such a subjectivity can be only hinted at by those who remain between impurity and purity.

Perhaps to re-emphasize his own half-pure state, Thoreau follows this meditation on chastity with a fishing interlude. "Hark! I hear a rustling of the leaves," the Hermit announces in "Brute Neighbors." "Is it some ill-fed village hound yielding to the instinct of the chase? or the lost pig which is said to be in these woods, whose tracks I saw after the rain?" he asks in playful parody of the "long ago lost" hound, horse, and dove. No, not the hound or the pig but a fellow poet appears, the first of his "brute neighbors" to arrive (223). Wishing to continue his meditation, the Hermit ponders whether to "go to heaven or a-fishing" (224), and he alludes again to the earlier disclosure of loss: "My thoughts have left no track, and I cannot find the path again" (224). By opting for fishing, he affirms the advantage of earthly re-creation over heavenly meditation, for—inspired by the eyes of a young partridge—he seeks both the "purity of infancy" and a "wisdom clarified by experience" (227).

From this point on, references in *Walden* to forest dogs and hounds signal Thoreau's self-avowed evolution toward a more chaste form of subjectivity. His narrative of the care of the self suggests the potential for others—animals as well as people—to become chaste. In "Winter Animals," for example, he brings together foxes, hounds, and men to represent the possibility of chastity as a practice of personal freedom. Reporting that sometimes at night he hears foxes in search of game, "barking raggedly and demoniacally like forest dogs," he speculates that they, "as well as men," might one day undergo evolution; they might be "laboring with some anxiety, or seeking expression, struggling for light and to be dogs outright and run freely in the streets" (273). He then explicitly links the foxes' potential with humanity's prospects: "They seemed to me to be rudimental, burrowing men, still standing on their defense, awaiting their transformation" (273). Simply to await transformation, however, is far from adequate, as Thoreau implies in another episode involving hounds. "In dark winter mornings, or in short winter afternoons," he reports, he "sometimes [hears] a pack of hounds threading all the woods with hounding cry and yelp, unable to resist the instinct of the chase, and the note of the hunting-horn at intervals proving that man was in the rear" (276). In this instance, the hounds are victimized by their own senses—and men, doubly so, bringing up the rear as they do.

Three more stories, following in quick succession, use hounds to reinforce the view that humanity can assimilate its hound/hunter stage by learning to direct the senses. Thoreau first relates a story told to him by a hunter. This hunter once saw "a fox pursued by hounds burst out on to Walden when the ice was covered with shallow puddles, run part way across, and then return to the same shore"; when the hounds returned, they had "lost the scent" (277). In the next two stories, Thoreau brings the theme of the hounds back to himself. "Sometimes a pack hunting by themselves would pass by my door, and circle round my house, and yelp and hound without regarding me, as if afflicted by a species of madness, so that nothing could divert them from pursuit." They would continue their circling until they found a new scent, "for a wise hound will forsake every thing else for this" (277). The fox-chasing hounds' inability to follow the scent and the hunting pack's mad pursuit of a new scent signify the lot of creatures wholly dependent on the senses as a way of knowing.

In his third story, not surprisingly, Thoreau distinguishes himself from a man content to remain hound-like: "One day a man came to my hut from Lexington to inquire after his hound that made a large track, and had been hunting for a week by himself. But I fear that he was not the wiser for all I told him, for every time I attempted to answer his questions he interrupted me by asking 'What do you do here?' He had lost a dog, but found a man" (277). This man's incomprehension of Thoreau's endeavor to confront life ethically shows him to be even more lost than his hound—or shows that it is he, not the hound, who is lost.

Thoreau relates two more stories involving the figures of the hound and the potential for a more chaste subjectivity. The first is another hunter's story. Unlike the hunter who has lost not only his hound but also himself, this man seems able to comprehend Thoreau's life at Walden, for it was his custom to "come to bathe in Walden once every year," at which time, Thoreau notes, he "looked in upon me" (277). This hunter describes an encounter with "an old hound and her three pups in full pursuit, hunting on their own account" (278). While resting in the woods one day, the man suddenly spied a fox under pursuit and killed it, even as the "demoniac cry" of the hounds resounded all around him. "At length the old hound burst into view with muzzle to the ground, and snapping the air as if possessed, and ran directly to the rock; but spying the dead fox she suddenly ceased her hounding, as if struck dumb with amazement, and walked round and round him in silence; and one by one her pups arrived, and, like their mother, were sobered into silence by mystery"(278–79). They remained silent even after the "mystery" was solved by the appearance of the hunter.

This story foreshadows the last of the hound allusions in "Winter Animals." Here again, silence and mystery are elevated to thematic status, but this time it is Thoreau himself who confuses the hounds. "At midnight, when there was a moon," he recalls, "I sometimes met with hounds in my path prowling about the woods, which would skulk out of my way, as if afraid, and stand silent amid the bushes till I had passed" (280). Thus, his transformative self-stylization has already begun and is reflected in the hounds' perplexity. It seems to him that he is not recognized by the creatures who symbolize for him the most primitive animal nature. After this, Thoreau reports no more reversions to unchecked sensuality. He loses some of the fear (expressed in "Higher Laws") that "we are such gods or demigods only as fauns and satyrs, the divine allied to the beasts, the creature of appetite" (220), as he begins learning to channel the wild or sublime into the good or beautiful.

A final reference to dogs in *Walden* dispels any illusion of full transformation, either personal or collective. Rebutting the opinion "dinning in our ears" that, compared to the ancients or to

the Elizabethans, Americans are "intellectual dwarfs," Thoreau
declares that a "living dog is better than a dead lion" (325–26).
Thus he reaffirms the gradualism of his proposed evolution toward a chaste and free humanity, an evolution that requires ongoing exercises of purification. We can see in *Walden*'s references
to hounds Thoreau's cumulative movement away from being
chased by his senses and toward becoming chaste through stylization of the senses.

*L*ook at the teamster on the highway, wending to market by
day or night; does any divinity stir within him? His highest
duty to fodder and water his horses! What is his destiny to him
compared with the shipping interests?" In this example (in
"Economy") of a commercially driven but spiritually direction-
less teamster, the horse represents the limitations of the collective
institutions of commerce and of the habits, customs, and conventions they enforce. The person who bows to commercial gods is
enslaved by commercial ventures and imprisoned by low ethical
aspiration. Thoreau comments that it is "hard to have a southern
overseer; it is worse to have a northern one; but worst of all
when you are the slave-driver of yourself." (7).

Throughout *Walden*, the figure of the horse signifies the forms
of surveillance and self-surveillance inherent in capitalist technology and in the corresponding technologies of the deployment of
sexuality. Just as the hound represents the knowledge of the
senses at the level of survival, the horse represents the knowledge
of the intellect at the level of technology. The image of a horse
with a rider connotes a strong tension between the two: the
horse is harnessed by its rider, but the rider may be led or
thrown by the horse. Although Thoreau associates the horse
with a stage of liberty and ethical-aesthetic development higher
than that of the hunter, he acknowledges the truth of Emerson's
observation: "Things are in the saddle and ride mankind."

That it is a bay horse Thoreau seeks is significant, for the
word *bay* carries at least four relevant meanings and thus under-

scores the multiplicity of language. In addition to referring to a reddish brown color in a horse, *bay* links the hound and the horse by evoking *Walden*'s recurrent baying dogs: the horse as a figure of human development toward chastity remains *at bay*. Furthermore, the word *bay* suggests enclosure, as of a body of water surrounded on three sides by land. Several of the bays Thoreau refers to in "The Pond in Winter" are so enclosed by bars that they appear to be "independent pond[s]." Here, enclosure serves to reveal nature's mysteries when Thoreau uses the bars in his formula to calculate the depth of the pond. He admits, however, that such formulae are frequently better in theory than in practice because streams or islands tend to throw off the calculation. Finally, the kind of *bay* Thoreau ultimately seeks is the laurel wreath bestowed on a poet. In this he differs from other human beings, most of whom settle for "bays of poesy": "It is true, we are such poor navigators that our thoughts, for the most part, stand off and on upon a harborless coast, are conversant only with the bights of the bays of poesy, or steer for the public ports of entry, and go into the dry docks of science, where they merely refit for this world, and no natural currents concur to individualize them" (292).

Four additional references to horses appear in "Economy." Three sound an alarm at the dangers of conformity—of being formed by social institutions and conventions; the fourth comments on the stage of human development signified by the horse. Like earlier references to the hound, these center on clothing, shelter, news, and work. However, they approach these subjects not in terms of mastery of the senses but on the level of social conformity and self-surveillance.

In the first reference, Thoreau contrasts his business venture at Walden—his trade with the "Celestial Empire"—with the ventures of those "led oftener by the love of novelty, and a regard for the opinions of men, in procuring it, than by a true utility" (21). He uses clothing as a symbol for commercial, as opposed to ethical, success and satirizes "kings and queens who wear a suit but once" and "cannot know the comfort of wearing a suit that fits. They are no better than wooden horses to hang the clean clothes on" (21). In this case, the horse as a lifeless apparatus—a clothes rack—represents an obstacle to the care of the chaste self: an obstacle that arises when one accepts the terms of social rank as signs of ethical selfhood. Thus, the wooden horse is to a live horse what social servitude is to ethical freedom.

In the next example, Thoreau points out the importance of moving to the stage of development signified by the horse. Noting that humanity learned first where to find and later how to construct shelters, he likens the development of the species to that of the individual. "We may imagine a time," he writes, "when in the infancy of the human race, some enterprising mortal crept into a hollow in a rock for shelter. Every child begins the world again, to some extent, and loves to stay outdoors, even in wet and cold. It plays house, as well as horse, having an instinct for it" (28). The child's play at house and horse represents a potential step beyond the hunting stage. On the other hand, it falls short of the aesthetic stage represented by the turtledove, for Thoreau warns that the advance from huts to buildings of stone may make "our lives . . . domestic in more senses than we think" (28). The poet, he remarks, "did not speak so much from under a roof, or the saint dwell there so long" (28). For Thoreau, as the next section of this chapter will show, the poet, like the dove, requires no overhead shelter and indeed desires none, for each wishes to be closer to the "celestial bodies" (28).

Thoreau's antagonism toward domesticity, which reinscribes the longstanding masculinist denigration of all that is associated with women and children, shows how his challenge to the construction of masculinity remains implicated in a binary opposition between masculinity and femininity. This opposition informs his distinction between the "mother tongue," which he describes as "commonly transitory, a sound, a tongue, a dialect merely, almost brutish" and the "father tongue," which represents the "maturity and experience" of the mother tongue, "a reserved and select expression, too significant to be heard by the ear" (101). To the extent that his conceptualization of aesthetic ethical development is constructed through derision of women or through their relegation to a less developed stage, it participates in the binary sexual system of patriarchy and promotes the Victorian ideology of gender-based separation of the public and private spheres.

Nevertheless, as we have seen, *Walden* challenges several features of nineteenth-century bourgeois masculinity. With alternating praise of solitude and sociality, for example, it problematizes the masculinist impulse either to control the public sphere or to escape the private one by "lighting out for the territory." And in performing the everyday tasks of domesticity, Thoreau provides an exemplary challenge to the view that these tasks are women's work. Most importantly, his remark that "before we can adorn our houses with beautiful objects the walls must be stripped, and our lives must be stripped, and beautiful housekeeping and beautiful living be laid for a foundation" suggests not so much contempt for domesticity per se as for bourgeois domesticity and perhaps an appreciation for nakedness. (38). By "stripping" away excess ornament, one renounces consumerism precisely so that one can *acquire* an aesthetic self. And it is worth recalling that *Walden*'s hopeful conclusion evokes a domestic scene, around a kitchen table, in fact, from which a "strong and beautiful bug" emerges after a long period of dormancy (333).

In his third horse reference, a critique of the technology of communication, Thoreau argues that many "modern improvements" are not worthy of the name. "We are eager to tunnel under the Atlantic and bring the old world some weeks nearer to the new," he observes, adding sarcastically: "Perchance the first news that will leak through into the broad, flapping American ear will be that the Princess Adelaide has the whooping cough" (52). He then sums up his position with the comment that, "after all, the man whose horse trots a mile a minute does not carry the most important message" (52). Notwithstanding its phenomenal speed record, this horse conveys Thoreau's skepticism about what is taken for progress in a developing society.

In "Economy" Thoreau uses the figure of the horse to expose the dangers even of "necessary work," particularly that involving the labor of animals; too often, Thoreau suggests, such work is arranged to make workers animal-like. "*I* should never have broken a horse or bull and taken him to board for any work he might do for me," Thoreau explains, "for fear I should become a horse-man or a herds-man merely" (56). Admitting that, at least sometimes, "society seems to be the gainer by so doing," he asks pointedly whether we are "certain that what is one man's gain is not another's loss, and that the stable boy has equal cause with his master to be satisfied?" (56). Especially questionable is any unnecessary work performed through animal labor, for in practice only "a few do all the exchange work with the oxen, or, in other words, become the slaves of the strongest" (57). Although he had implied as much in the passage about the teamster and his horse, he now unequivocally states that "man thus not only works for the animal within him, but, for a symbol of this, he works for the animal without him" (57).

These references to the horse tend to dispel the illusion of inevitable progress through increasingly complex societal arrangements and technical innovations. However, *Walden* also explores the promise of technology to forge a network of shared enterprise and knowledge that could "make our civilization a blessing" (40). "Sounds" approaches the "Iron Horse" in a spirit of celebration of this "traveling demigod." When Thoreau hears the "iron horse make the hills echo with his snort like thunder, shaking the earth with his feet, and breathing fire and smoke from his nostrils, (what kind of winged horse or fiery dragon they will put into the new Mythology I don't know,) it seems as if the earth had got a race now worthy to inhabit it" (116). But this ode to technological power, already admitting a parenthetical doubt, is abruptly interrupted by a complaint: "If all were as it seems, and men made the elements their servants for noble ends! If the cloud that hangs over the engine were the perspiration of heroic deeds, or as beneficent to men as that which floats over the farmer's fields, then the elements and Nature herself would cheerfully accompany men in their errands and be their escort" (116). The repeated conditionals in this passage fuse ambitious hopes with doubt about their potential for realization.

Deeply ambivalent about the locomotive, Thoreau pursues the horse metaphor at some length:

> The stabler of the iron horse was up early this winter morning by the light of the stars amid the mountains, to fodder and harness his steed. . . . All day the fire-steed flies over the country, stopping only that his master may rest, and I am awakened by his tramp and defiant snort at midnight, when in some remote glen in the woods he fronts the elements incased in ice and snow; and he will reach his stall only with the morning star, to start once more on his travels without rest or slumber. . . . If the enterprise were as heroic and commanding as it is protracted and unwearied! (117)

The metaphor of the railroad points to an unmet human potential: to the extent that the railroad orders and regulates the lived world of the populace, the "stabler" has been stabled. As Thoreau points out, to "do things 'railroad fashion' is now the byword" (118). The arrivals and departures of the railway cars are "now the epochs in the village day" (117). Hence, the railway system has dramatically altered social relations: time has been made to comply with the train schedule, and geographic space has changed—locations once formidably distant are now accessible and seem to demand travel to them.

Thoreau's warnings about the hazards of the locomotive are not anticommercial; in the next passage, he praises commerce for its "enterprise and bravery." What he cautions against is technology used unreflectively, so that it ruins the environment and regulates the population. Perhaps nowhere is this more clear or poignant than in his words about the locomotive's detrimental effects on Walden. "That devilish Iron Horse, whose ear-rending neigh is heard throughout the town," he protests, "has muddied the Boiling Spring with his foot, and he it is that has browsed off all the woods on Walden Shore; that Trojan Horse, with a thousand men in his belly, introduced by mercenary Greeks!" (192). The locomotive is a potentially noble product of ignoble men—men whose practices have formed them as normalized, mercenary subjects rather than as aesthetically ethical subjects. His association of the flying "fire-steed" with Pegasus, signifier of poetic inspiration, is a plea for greater awareness of the consequences of technology.

The technological stage can, nonetheless, develop into an aesthetic one, as Thoreau indicates in two subsequent references to the horse. First he mentions the poet's winged horse in the context of a "winged cat" about which he had heard, pointing out how appropriate it would be for a poet to have such a rare creature, "for why should not a poet's cat be winged as well as his horse?" (233). As I shall argue more fully in the next section, wings and winged creatures signal not only the potential of the human species to refine itself but also Thoreau's own development into more chaste subjectivity. In the second reference, Thoreau again indicates his personal movement from the canine to the equine stage, a movement designated earlier by the silence of the hounds in his presence. This passage (in "Spring," which describes the end of his first year at Walden) is notable for its discussion of the interplay between life and death and for the attitude it proposes toward life's contingencies. In it, Thoreau reports coming upon a "dead horse in the hollow by the path to [his] house" (318). He declares that the horse, despite a decaying odor so rank that it forced him to go out of his way, is a sign of nature's "strong appetite and inviolable health" (318). Cataloguing other instances of parasitism and destructiveness in nature and society, he responds in the Stoic tradition, observing that, given our "liability to accident, we must see how little account is to be made of it" (318). Such an attitude resists the will to determinate truth and the will to power over death, both integral to the deployment of sexuality and the construction of masculinity it prescribes.

This train of thought, with its chastening conclusion, demonstrates again the vitality of the wild for technological creativity. It shows how the wild, represented by the dead horse, might lead us toward the good of Stoic wisdom or, correspondingly, how the senses might contribute to the development of the intellect and the imagination. As in earlier discussions, generative energy is crucial. In humanity's progress from the hound stage to the horse stage, in which the senses are assimilated and channeled toward the intellect, this generative energy converts hunting prowess into technological achievement. In the dove stage, the generative energy transforms the wild into an etho-poetic selfhood: "At the same time that we are earnest to explore and learn all things, we require that all things be mysterious and unexplorable, that land and sea be infinitely wild, unsurveyed and unfathomed by us because unfathomable" (317–18). Our inability to master the wild conceptually or in any other way is essential to its generative function for us. Instead of taking bio-power's characteristic stance that humanity should control nature (and, by extension, all existence), Thoreau celebrates the impossibility of such control. "We need to witness our own limits transgressed, and some life pasturing freely where we never wander" (318). Thus, these passages show how, in Thoreau's aesthetics of liberty, sublime disruptions of normalizing order generate the beautiful in the form of artistry of self and society.

The dead horse signifies Thoreau's entry into the aesthetic stage of his personal development. With the fable of the Artist of Kouroo in the final chapter of *Walden*, he suggests what it would mean to realize this stage. The Artist, carving his staff, is so devoted to his work that it seems as though time has stopped: as though "no more time [has] elapsed than is required for a single scintillation from the brain of Brahma to fall on and inflame the tinder of a mortal brain" (327). An inflamed imagination enables one to build "castles in the air," but imaginary constructions are justified only if one puts "foundations under them." The care of the chaste self according to an aesthetics of liberty provides such a foundation: one needs a coalition of the senses, the intellect, and the imagination in order to continually re-create the world and oneself. Furthermore, such re-creation can be learned from example. "When one man has reduced a fact of the imagination to be a fact to his understanding, I forsee that all men will at length establish their lives on that basis" (11).

While the closing chapter focuses primarily on the surpassing merits of an aesthetic life, a final reference to the horse reminds readers how different such a life is from their own. Thoreau names some trivial concerns of his contemporaries about "costume and manners" and the news of the day, then uses the example of a bogged-down horse to illustrate the downward pull of conventional or unquestioning knowledge:

> We read that the traveller asked the boy if the swamp before him had a hard bottom. The boy replied that it had. But presently the traveller's horse sank in up to the girths, and he observed to the boy, "I thought you said that this bog had a hard bottom." "So it has," answered the latter, "but you have not got half way to it yet." So it is with the bogs and quicksands of society; but he is an old boy that knows it. (330)

Thus, Thoreau hints at the aesthetic life, only to reveal to his readers the extent of their unaesthetic, or anesthetized, existence. He advises them how to work toward poetic purity: "Drive a nail home and clinch it so faithfully that you can wake up in the night and think of your work with satisfaction—a work at which you would not be ashamed to invoke the Muse" (330).

The tale of the traveller's horse underscores both the possibility of attaining chastity and the danger of stopping short at the level of social conformity and technological regulation. Thoreau goes beyond this, however, with his imagery of the dove, which represents the higher pursuits of the aesthetic life.

A lthough only four explicit references to doves appear in *Walden*, numerous allusions to winged creatures combine with them to portray the stage of development that comes out of and goes beyond those of hound and horse. Dove imagery represents knowledge of the imagination and an aesthetic form of existence. Though Thoreau sketches this stage as the apogee of aesthetic-ethical development, he points out its counter-tendencies as well. The dove, for example, is a classic symbol of peace and spirituality but is also capable of fierce battle with its own species. Thus, Thoreau gives the turtledove meanings ranging from the mourning dove, an evocation of sorrow, to the Holy Dove, an evocation of hope.

Early in *Walden*, Thoreau associates the figure of the dove with aesthetics and purity. Recommending that we follow the poet and the saint in spending "more of our days and nights without any obstruction between us and the celestial bodies," he observes that "birds do not sing in caves, nor do doves cherish their innocence in dovecots"(28). Thus, innocence is cherished only if it has a social dimension whereby the innocent goes out into the world in an effort to bespeak the wisdom acquired from interaction with nature.

From start to finish, *Walden* offers a myriad of bird allusions that both prompt and chart the movement from the wild to the good. The first involves a "stray goose" that Thoreau hears "groping about over the pond and cackling as if lost, or like the spirit of the fog" (42). The goose, like the hunter in search of his hounds, illustrates the primitive condition of humanity. Seeing a snake in its "torpid state," content to remain at the bottom of the pond, Thoreau remarks that "for a like reason men remain in their present low and primitive condition; but if they should feel the influence of the spring of springs arousing them, they would of necessity rise to a higher and more ethereal life" (41). In Thoreau's aesthetics of liberty, to rise to an ethereal (or dovelike) life is to refine oneself in such a way that celestiality informs one's earthly life. According to this view, chastity is liberty.

The birds and winged creatures in *Walden* furnish an indirect yet scrupulously kept account of Thoreau's own rise to a more ethereal life through the care of the chaste self. In "Economy," he compares the "fitness in a man's building his own house" to a "bird's building its own nest" and goes as far as to speculate whether, if such work were done regularly, "the poetic faculty would be universally developed, as birds universally sing when they are so engaged" (46). In the next line, however, this crystalline hope is shattered: most people are like "cowbirds and cuckoos, which lay their eggs in nests which other birds have built and cheer no traveller with their chattering and unmusical notes" (46). The fact that Thoreau *does* construct his own house places him with the more melodious birds, not with the majority of cowbird-like human beings. He repeats this identification in the second chapter with his next two references to birds. The first, restating the epigram of the title page (first edition), proposes "to brag as lustily as chanticleer in the morning." In the second, Thoreau notes that his abode makes him "neighbor to the birds; not by having imprisoned one, but having caged [himself] near them" (85). His use of the word "cage" reminds us that, despite having made his own shelter, he is encumbered by it.

In "Sounds," amidst several brief references to hawks, wild pigeons, partridges, and whippoorwills, a longer passage on owls suggests the melancholy dimension of the pursuit of an aesthetics of liberty. The mourning strains of screech owls and the serenade of a hooting owl remind Thoreau less of the music of the poets than of the wail of a "graveyard ditty." Yet their "doleful" cries seem to be the "dark and tearful side of music, the regrets and sighs that would fain be sung" (124). The owls, then, represent the mourning also associated with the turtledove of his search—the search for knowledge and experience that includes the darker realities of life.

At this stage in the narrative of Thoreau's personal development, sightings of birds other than the lost turtledove are reminders of his half-pure state. He alludes to his state of partial cultivation in a passage that describes his bean-field, where he often sees birds. The field, he reports, was "the connecting link between wild and cultivated fields; as some states are civilized, and others half-civilized, and others savage or barbarian, so my field was, though not in a bad sense, a half-cultivated field"

(158). Sometimes as he worked in his bean-field, he would spy overhead a nighthawk, an "aerial brother of the wave which he sails over and surveys" (159). At other times he would watch a "pair of hen-hawks circling high in the sky, alternately soaring and descending, approaching and leaving one another, as if they were the imbodiment of my own thoughts" (159). Occasionally he spotted the traces of wild pigeons (similar to the turtledove) or witnessed their "passage from this wood to that, with a slight quivering winnowing sound and carrier haste" (159). These sightings from his "half-cultivated field" appear almost exactly at the midpoint of *Walden*.

If one counts by chapters, "Baker Farm" marks the second half of *Walden*. It ends with a reference to the Holy Dove and a warning that, to really "rise in the world," one needs wings. Thoreau describes John Field mired in his peat-bogging farm and follows with four stanzas of poetry that lament Baker Farm and its too-tame residents. The fourth stanza tries to incite a bogged-down humanity to action:

> Come ye who love,
>   And ye who hate,
> Children of the Holy Dove,
>   And Guy Faux of the state,
> And hang conspiracies
>   From the tough rafters of the trees! (208)

As children of the wild (Guy Fawkes) and of the good (the Holy Dove), they must fight against forces that suppress their generative energies, forces both inside and outside (on the rafters and in the trees), so that they might become more chaste. Although one might expect that an Irishman would be ready for rebellion, Thoreau doubts John Field's ability to rebel against his stagnant existence. Field, he concludes, is unlikely "to rise in this world, he nor his posterity, till their wading webbed bog-trotting feet get *talaria* to their heels" (209). In "Higher Laws," Thoreau contrasts Field's custom of "com[ing] tamely home at night" with his own "savage delight" in the wild, which gives him energy for practices for the transformation of self and society.

From "Higher Laws" forward, Thoreau depicts his personal transformation as underway. He symbolizes this self-transformation in "Brute Neighbors" by reporting turtledoves in the woods. During his customary noonday break, he writes "There too the turtle-doves sat over the spring, or fluttered from bough to bough of the soft white pines over my head" (228). In this fourth and last of his explicit references to doves, he notes that they number among the many creatures that "live wild and free though secret in the woods" (227). Their wildness and freedom represent the kind of generative energy he seeks. Once again, however, the promise of attainment of the chaste life is qualified by a reminder of how difficult that goal is; the sighting of the turtledove is followed by a battle between red and black ants, the "red republicans on the one hand, and the black imperialists on the other" (229). Like doves and ants, human beings are prone to fight fiercely against their own kind. But this fighting is necessary if the republican ants are to overthrow the forces of imperialism. Presumably, republicanism is the historical-political equivalent of the transition from the equine stage of development to the winged, poetic stage.

The next reference to a bird points to the precariousness of Thoreau's chaste selfhood and also reveals the multiple meanings of winged life itself. In the loon-chase episode at the end of "Brute Neighbors," Thoreau confronts the limits of human knowledge: When the loon plunges deep into the pond, "no wit [can] divine" its whereabouts. Only when it resurfaces and sounds its "demonic laughter" or "utter[s] a long-drawn unearthly howl" is he able to catch another glimpse. When a sudden storm coincides with the loon's cry, Thoreau is as "impressed as if it were the prayer of the loon answered, and his god was angry with me" (236). He leaves the loon "disappearing far away on the tumultuous surface" (236).

This unsuccessful pursuit precedes Thoreau's encounters with the hounds that fall silent before him and the dead horse beside the path. The loon episode, an instance of the process of the "elevation of the mean" portrayed in "Higher Laws," reveals Thoreau's own wildness in the process of acquiring chastity. Having left behind the savage chase after animal flesh, he now pursues, with measured senses, this "stately bird," this harbinger of the turtledove. His resources, however, may still be insufficient; in any event, he admits that he is not yet ready to comprehend fully the loon's wildness. Nor does he exhibit the mature understanding that leads him to remark later, in the account of the dead horse, that "we need to witness our own limits transgressed" (318). That later recognition enkindles a renewed desire for chastity, but here, exasperated by the loon, he settles for hours of watching ducks "tack and veer" on Walden's surface.

In contrast to this reported failure to follow the loon, *Walden*'s penultimate chapter ("Spring") recounts a number of successful sightings—including one of a loon. Harbingers of the dove abound. The "first sparrow of spring" signifies the "year beginning with younger hope than ever" (310). Thoreau hears a chorus of birdsongs all around. The song of a robin in the distance encourages him to wonder whether he "could ever find the twig he sits upon!" "I mean *he*, I mean *the twig*," he stresses, pointing to the "unfathomable," which spurs us to transgress our limits (318). On the twenty-ninth of April, he catches sight of a nighthawk spiraling upward, alone and needing no companion "but the morning." Following this event, which he reports with awe, is the incident of the dead horse, which, in turn, is followed by sightings of the loon, "the whippoorwill, the brown-thrasher, the veery, the wood pewee, the chewink and other birds" (319).

The onrush of spring and birds unmistakably lifts Thoreau toward aesthetic concerns. In his "Conclusion," he writes:

I learned this, at least, by my experiment; that if one advances confidently in the direction of his dreams, and endeavors to live the life which he has imagined, he will meet with a success unexpected in common hours. He will put some things behind, will pass an invisible boundary; new, universal, and more liberal laws

will begin to establish themselves around and within him; or the
old laws be expanded, and interpreted in his favor in a more liberal sense, and he will live with the license of a higher order of
beings. (323–24).

Hence, imagination emerges as vital to an aesthetics of liberty in
the care of the chaste self. By enabling humanity to speculate
about an aesthetic order of being, imagination guides ethical
practices of liberty.

In keeping with this connection between imagination and a
higher or more chaste existence, the final parable of *Walden* ex-
horts readers toward the "winged life." Recalling "a strong and
beautiful bug" that crawled out from the dead wood of a farmer's table after having been dormant in egg form for sixty years,
Thoreau asks, "Who knows what beautiful and winged life,
whose egg has been buried for ages under many concentric layers
of woodenness in the dead dry life of society, . . . may unexpect-
edly come forth from amidst society's most trivial and hanselled
furniture, to enjoy its perfect summer life at last!" (333). This
final allusion to winged life concludes with the question "who
knows?" and thus recalls the declaration in "Higher Laws" that a
man "shall not know" if he is chaste. Thoreau is still on the
trail, along with a few others mentioned at the outset: the "one
or two who [have] heard the hound, and the tramp of the horse,
and even seen the dove disappear behind a cloud" (17).

T hroughout *Walden*, then, the attainment of chastity remains
an indeterminate prospect, both for Thoreau and for human
beings collectively. Even while Thoreau presents himself as an
increasingly chaste chasseur of an etho-poetic life, he underscores
the need to continue the search for the dove and all it represents.
And despite his progress in individual transformation, he finds
that collective transformation lags behind. The intricate structuring device of the hound-horse-dove web not only reinforces the
theme of continued struggle but suggests a disparity between

Thoreau and most others. References to the hound far outnumber those to the horse and the dove. Furthermore, Thoreau links the canine and equine metaphors most often to other people or to society in general, reserving the dove and bird metaphors for himself. In this way he suggests that the majority of human beings live cognitively and experientially through their senses, that some have refined their senses and cultivated their intellects, and that only a few experience life and conduct themselves aesthetically. Although he places himself in the last group, he acknowledges the need to continue training himself aesthetically.

Supporting the theme of endlessness in the care of the chaste self is Thoreau's report that he left Walden in the summer. A number of critics treat *Walden* as though Thoreau had departed in the spring and emphasize thereby the rebirth and triumph connoted by that season.[7] But Thoreau concludes with a discussion of summer, stressing the significance of that season in terms of continued rambling. "And so the seasons went rolling on into summer, as one rambles into higher and higher grass," he writes, adding that he "finally left Walden September 6th, 1847" (319). Having noted his "accidental" arrival on July 4th, 1845—a day which in retrospect becomes a personal declaration of independence from the daily routines of normalizing masculinity—he depicts himself, at the end, again in summer, the season in which one's senses, intellect, and imagination are most fully attuned. As he has already said, "a taste for the beautiful is most cultivated out of doors" (38). *Walden* concludes, therefore, not with an assurance of chastity but rather with an affirmation of the value of acquiring and caring for a chaste self.

CHAPTER FOUR

Fostering the Freedom of the Self through the Liberty of the Other: Agee and Evans's *Let Us Now Praise Famous Men* and the Ethical Aesthetics of Counterespionage

*E*merson once advised a group of divinity students that "the preacher should be a poet smit with [the] love of the harmonies of moral nature" (*Journals* 471). We might imagine Jefferson, Fuller, and Thoreau proclaiming their agreement and, like Emerson, extending that advice to all Americans. These writers all describe aesthetic-ethical existence so enticingly that their works endure to this day. Yet from the perspective of contemporary critical theory, their aspirations toward an ideal accord might well be dismissed as utopian. More importantly, such aspirations might be read as denying diversity in the name of a common humanity.

In *Let Us Now Praise Famous Men,* James Agee and Walker Evans problematize an aesthetics of liberty based on Enlightenment principles of universality and harmony in human morality—but they accomplish this without relinquishing the value of an ethical aesthetics of life. Instead, they reaccent the notion of harmony, constructing an aesthetics of liberty that recognizes and honors human diversity and the contradictoriness of existence. Throughout the work, we find the ethical perspectives characteristic of Jefferson, Fuller, and Thoreau: the insistence that ethics and aesthetics are co-constitutive; the equal valuation of the senses, the emotions, the intellect, and the imagination for purposes of ethical self-stylization; the appropriation of a religious idiom to describe the physical-cultural world and its inhabitants; the use of the first-person form to stress each individual's potential for ethical artistry; the application of an aesthetics of sublimity and beauty; and the overt incitement to ethical-political action, tempered by an acknowledgment of life's deep ambiguity. But *Let Us* syncopates the harmonies found in the works of Jefferson, Fuller, and Thoreau with the disharmonies of the social world. *Let Us* proposes an ethics informed by twentieth-century destabilizations of truth, aesthetics, language, and objectivity. By drawing on the artistic innovations of their time, particularly in film and sound recording, Agee and Evans challenge the univocal and totalizing practices of disciplinary forms of visual, audio, and linguistic representation.

In this chapter I will show how Agee and Evans reframe self-stylization as an ethical practice by making the freedom of the other integral to the freedom of the self. In the photographs and verbal depictions of the lives of three tenant farm families, they illustrate how the meanings and values of one's own life depend on one's understanding of the meanings and values of others' lives. To be sure, over the decades between the Civil War and the Great Depression, a number of American writers eloquently articulated the importance of acknowledging others' values as part of one's own ethical stance; Walt Whitman, William James, and Jane Addams are perhaps best known for this. But to my mind, *Let Us* is the most significant rethinking of the issues that distinguish this American ethical tradition.

Let Us reformulates an aesthetics of liberty in three important ways. First, it fully elaborates the view that self-stylization is enhanced by the capacity to respect the sometimes unfamiliar lives and values of others. Second, it makes clear the relationship between ethics and power relations, showing how tenantry as an economic and social practice problematizes America's proclaimed democratic freedoms and demonstrating how oppressive power relations operate through the bodies of individuals. And third, it raises issues of surveillance crucial to our understanding of the relationship between normalizing power and an aesthetics of liberty, showing how surveillance technologies—from the panopticon to photography to electronic monitoring devices—are the material conditions of a self-other ethics.

In the preface to *Let Us*, Agee explains the impetus for the book: "It was our business to prepare, for a New York magazine, an article on cotton tenantry in the United States, in the form of a photographic and verbal record of the daily living and environment of an average white family of tenant farmers" (xiii). Agee as journalist and Evans as photographer were "on loan from the Federal Government" (xiii), enlisted by the normalizing forces of twentieth-century power/knowledge, which treat human beings as both the preeminent objects of study and the preeminent studiers of human objects. Agee writes that, from the outset, this project struck him as a "curious piece of work" (xiii), and in the book's list of persons and places, he humorously identifies himself as a spy and Evans as a counterspy. But in light of the proliferation in that era of the normalizing bio-powers of the human sciences, a government-sponsored examination of regional poverty was not in the least curious. What *was* curious, as Agee points out, was that he and Evans were selected for such an assignment.[1]

Let Us is a testimony to their resistance against what Agee calls "obscene" prying into the lives of human beings. Their assignment was to display "these lives before another group of human beings, in the name of science, of 'honest journalism' (whatever that paradox may mean), of humanity, of social fearlessness, for money, and for a reputation of crusading and for unbias which, when skillfully enough qualified, is exchangeable at any bank for money" (7). Their book is a record of counterespionage against the forces of journalistic and governmental surveillance. It exposes the conventional conceptual categories of the human sciences embraced by documentary journalism, which acts in concert with capitalism's commodification of one set of human beings for the consumption of another.[2] *Let Us* is, in Agee's words, "an effort in human actuality, in which the reader is no less centrally involved than the authors and those of whom they tell" (xvi). The book merges reader, author, and tenants in a collective and transactional form of selfhood—an I/we/us—that challenges claims of objectivity. It presents an aesthetic ethics that promotes personal and social responsibility as practices of freedom.

Agee and Evans's discursive and visual resistance to government and human-science surveillance might be billed as a counter-espionage musical production. Reading *Let Us* this way draws attention to the ways Agee and Evans use motion picture and musical forms of representation to disrupt their intelligence gathering mission. As a form of entertainment, the musical is an especially auspicious vehicle for such resistance to the claims of disciplinary power to represent objective reality. Just as a musical's interjection of songs in the narrative interrupts its illusion of reality, Evans and Agee's use of cinematic and musical devices dislodges any presumption of objectivity in their text. I will discuss these disruptive devices in the first part of this chapter and then will turn to Agee's explicit formulation of film and music as destabilizing modes of representation, particularly as applied to his prose. Finally, I propose that *Let Us* uses the devices of film and music to radically challenge the premises and practices of normalizing power/knowledge, especially those of traditional aesthetics and the social sciences.

Evans's photographic text opens the work deconstructively by refusing orthodox methods of documentary portraiture, for, even if the photographs record the "absolute, dry truth," as Agee proclaims they do, these uncaptioned truths appear as discrete entities whose implied relations to one another remain ambiguous. Evans's truths, in other words, are not offered as *the* Truth.[3] Furthermore, if one discerns beauty in these photographs—in the weathered face of the woman given the name "Annie Mae Gudger" (no real names are used) or in the vulnerable expressions of the children—it is not the time-honored classical form of beauty. It is, rather, the beauty in the way the texture of a woman's skin resembles the lines of the worn wood behind her or the beauty in her gaze of resistance; or it is the beauty evoked by the sight of the sound bodies of children who may become twisted and beaten down before they are grown. It is, in other words, a beauty derived less from harmony and proportion than from a sense of the discrepancy between that potential and the life-ravaging poverty that threatens it.

Agee's written text points explicitly to the unreliability of all claims to absolute truth and meaning. He states that no matter what truth he should utter, "of course it will be only a relative truth" (239). Such an assertion distinguishes him from Jefferson, Fuller, and Thoreau more by degree than by qualitative difference, but the distinction is important. Thoreau's insistence on the "infinite number of profiles" of a mountain, for example, is countered by his assumption that the mountain has "one form" (*Walden* 290–91). His view that nature's language is both "copious" and "standard" situates his discourse on two competing registers, one in which meaning is a human construction (hence his emphasis on infinite interpretability) and one in which meaning is fixed in nature (hence his valuation of Nature's Truth). These two registers remain in tension with one another throughout *Walden*. In *Let Us*, Agee and Evans treat meaning as a human construction in order to problematize the notion of univocal meaning and thereby force scrutiny of the determinations of class, race, and (to a lesser extent) gender enforced by normalizing power/knowledge mechanisms.

The segments of Book II entitled "ON THE PORCH" exemplify this stance. Agee renders the title "(ON THE PORCH: 1" with only the first half of a parenthesis, transgressing grammatical conventions to suggest an open-endedness of meaning. Reality, to be perceived as such, is constituted through the marking of boundaries—but that marking alters reality. There are no natural or absolute points of beginning or ending, but through the accepted artifice of the grammatical frame, one reduces reality to a parenthetical, ordered statement with its signs of closure. This title, with its single parenthesis, resists such enclosures and reductions of meaning. In addition, the colon at the end creates a sense of expectancy and prompts readers to await explanation or clarification. Thus engaged, however, the readers find in place of words a number, a subtitle enigmatic in its relation to the heading but still suggestively authorizing as an ordering device. Placed in the context of these uncertain relationships, or rather out of place in this context, the authority of encapsulating titles and numerical order is de-authorized, and reading is shown to be a transactional, meaning-making activity.

A separate section called "Colon" has no number in its title, which is followed instead by a colon-divided flood of words paying homage to human existence. Yet these words, Agee indicates, unavoidably screen off or defer the manuscript of what they attempt to describe. The absence of words after the colon of "(ON THE PORCH: 1" invites the "human co-operation" about which Agee writes in "Colon." "The most I can do," he states, "the most I can hope to do—is to make a number of physical entities as plain and vivid as possible, and to make a few guesses, a few conjectures; and to leave to you much of the burden of realizing in each of them what I have wanted to make clear of them as a whole: how each is itself; and how each is a shapener" (110). Seen in the light of this passage, *Let Us* becomes a metaphorical colon, awaiting various realizations through readers' interpretations—realizations that cannot be fixed in the text, nor in the textuality of life.[4]

Agee states in a note in "(ON THE PORCH: 2" that it was written "to stand as the beginning of a much longer book" (245). But as it appears in *Let Us,* it is "intended still in part as a preface or opening, but also as a frame and as an undertone and as the set stage and center of action, in relation to which all other parts of this volume are intended as flashbacks, foretastes, illuminations and contradictions" (245). This clause-upon-clause statement, comprising a series of metaphors which both contain and spill over meaning, is designed to say something, indeed many things, yet it defers any final say. In keeping with this design, the segment is divided into three sections that appear, respectively, near the beginning of the book, approximately in the center, and at the end. In keeping with the idea of the work as a musical, these three segments may be seen as three musical numbers that interrupt the narrative. Thus, "ON THE PORCH" may be read as one continuous piece or in installments over the course of the larger text. It is, in other words, a constructed beginning, center, and end—all at the same time. By reorienting narrative structure in this way, Agee challenges the linear logic of traditional narrative while providing a processive yet destabilized narrative.

Given this excursion into the radical unreliability of meaning, what prevents Agee's text from whirling into an epistemological void? Staving off nihilistic despair in Agee's discourse is the expressed belief that, even though human beings will never know "all of even the human truth," they should recognize that they "know a few things." Thus, while challenging spurious claims of objective knowledge, Book II also decries the absolutism of a relativist stance that denies all knowledge. Agee argues that beauty is knowable: that "plain objects and atmospheres have a sufficient intrinsic beauty and nature that it might be well if the describer became more rather than less shameless" (239). In other words, while Agee relinquishes the notion of a single standard or of certain meaning in nature or in texts, he retains the view that beauty is intrinsic to nature and therefore is accessible to the senses—even if the meanings of that accessibility cannot be fixed.

Agee sees art as a mode of cognition that transforms human capacities to know. And this is precisely its value for ethics. Science seeks to describe what is, art to transform the describer. Because the meanings of beauty are not fixed, Agee suggests, one can and ought to redefine beauty. At the same time, words are "artful dodges" at best. Thus, this art/life perspective announces itself as both dependent on and at odds with its medium: words. And, as with truth and language, the significance of human existence is not only undecidable but self-contradictory: doleful on the one hand, celebratory on the other. Over the course of the work, Evans's photographs and Agee's text mourn life's tragedies while exulting in its joys.

The pages of silent images that open the work mark a rupture between language and the world. By presenting his thirty-one photographs without titles or comments to explain them, Evans forces direct confrontation with the images. Through the photographs we enter the text with our eyes focused on images rather than on print. The experience is unlike that of words alone or that of images with identifying, classificatory labels. The physical character of the book, then, invites questions rather than providing instructions and thus disrupts the conventions of reading. By refusing to use captions, Evans creates the possibility of a reader-initiated dialogue between the people who see the images and those who "people" the photographs.

What kind of exchange might occur in this dialogue? Perhaps others have wondered, as I do, who, in their particularity, these people are. Perhaps others have cringed at the tenants' destitution, felt a redundancy of vacant eyes and tired, lean bodies. Yet, in part because of the title, but more because of the diffusion of light over the photographs, the wordless images seem to become icons. The faces, especially of the children, appear serene. This is not a freewheeling dialogue, for Evans's images guide viewers in certain ways. All of the photographs of the tenants are obviously posed: there is no implied claim that these are people going about their daily routine without an audience. Instead, the subjects "look back." As John Berger has written of Paul Strand's images, the "subject is looking at us; we are looking at the subject; it has been arranged like that" (46). The result of this frontality, Berger observes, is that the subjects become narrators and the photographer and subsequent viewers become listeners. Like Strand's portraits, Evans's subjects appear to say: "I am as you see me" (46). Each photograph emerges as a complex autobiographical statement, one that has been related by the subject of the photograph but is retold by Evans. Thus, the photographs

become Evans's imagistic personal narrative as well—his account
of his relationship to himself as photographer and to these individuals—an account that includes their relationships to themselves and each other.

The various first-person stories I read from these photographs
tell both of individual aloneness and of the closeness of individuals to each other, to the land, and to home. The first photograph depicts a man noticeable in his difference from the others.
His suit jacket and tie, the softness of his skin, his more substan-
tial body and the painted-over surface of the structure behind
him set him apart. Subsequent images show stubbly-bearded
men, women with wrinkled skin, children in ragged clothing,
gaunt bodies, and raw wood buildings. Three of the photographs are family portraits, and several close-ups of the children
show them touching one another. Nature as sublime landscape is
conspicuously absent, but one photograph of a dwelling demonstrates that the land, despite its depleted appearance, can sustain
some grass and trees; a chicken scratches the sandy soil behind
one of the houses. Here, then, is the texture of these lives as suggested in Evans's photographic text.

Only after reading Agee's Book II is one able to link (assigned) names with particular images. Upon returning to the
photographic text, we learn that it, like the discursive text, begins with the image of a landowner. Thus we have been introduced to the tenant families—the Gudgers, the Woods, and the
Ricketts—through the representation of one who frames their
lives, even as Evans and Agee have framed their lives photo-
graphically and textually. The photographic narrative tells a
story of separateness and closeness combined, moving from individual portraits of the Gudgers and of the empty rooms in their
house through an intermixture of separate and family portraits of
the Woods and their house, to a final family scene with Fred
Ricketts and three of his children singing together. The fourth-
to-last photograph raises the issue of photographic representation. It is a photograph of two photographs nailed somewhat
crookedly to an interior wall. One depicts a woman by herself;
the other is of four children. Unlike Evans's photographs, these

appear to have been taken by a family member or friend. With their presentation in *Let Us,* their place in family history becomes explicitly linked to public history, which is not, as tradition would have it, exclusively the place of military and political leaders.

The final three photographs are scenes of town. The first provides a stark contrast to the field-and-house spaces of the tenants. Here, a car-and-truck-lined street suggests the more comfortable lives of the landowners and storekeepers. The second photograph portrays a deserted area of town, suggestive of the ghost-town effects of the depression. The final photograph of the series, showing a two-story structure with the words "MAYORS OFFICE" above the door, presents pictorially several themes discussed in Book II. As an institution of the law, the mayor's office circumscribes the tenants' lives. The barred windows of the second story are dark, their upper portion shaded by the overhang of the roof. Large puddles several feet in front of the building capture the reflection of the building. Strikingly, the watery image reverses the words MAYORS OFFICE, creating a multiple signification and a suggestion that the structure—the architectural space of local law—has been overturned.[5]

Although Evans's images partake of the conventions of religious iconography, their presentation and context make them simultaneously iconic and iconoclastic. Like traditional icons, the portraits suggest a deific presence and invite viewers to worship that power. Yet, there are no depictions of orthodox deities or saints here; instead, deific presence is used to suggest human potentialities. In one photograph, a table shoved against a fireplace suggests a religious altar, but the metaphysical holiness of the "altar" is brought back to earth with a reminder of the requirements of human comfort: a pair of shoes is tucked below. As an iconoclast, Evans attempts to break false images on two fronts: he displaces the divine with the human even as he exposes the misery wrought by a humanly constructed social system.

According to Agee's preface, the "nominal subject" of the work is "North American cotton tenantry as examined in the daily living of three representative white tenant families" (xiv).

He goes on to point out that it is, "more essentially, . . . an independent inquiry into certain normal predicaments of human divinity" (xiv). Explaining in "Colon" what he means by human divinity, he describes the "human 'soul' " as "that which is angry, that which is wild, that which is untamable, that which is healthful and holy, that which is competent of all advantaging within hope of human dream," but also that which is "the most defenseless, the most easily and multitudinously wounded, frustrate [sic], prisoned, and nailed into a cheating of itself" (99–100). Throughout Book II of *Let Us,* Agee identifies human beings as divine because of their unfathomability and immortality. As Walker Evans commented about Agee, "After a while, in a round-about way, you discovered that, to him, human beings were at least possibly immortal and literally sacred souls" (xii).

The question whether Agee accepted the notion of life after death remains unanswered in *Let Us,* but the text is explicit about his view of humanity as sacred.[6] This view should not be confused with the orthodox religious notion of a sacred soul housed or imprisoned in a profane body. For Agee, human beings—body and "soul"—are sacred in their earthly existence. *Human* divinity breaks with both religious and humanistic views that claim absolute knowledge or define poverty as a necessary evil. Evans's apt phrase, "in a round-about way," describes the way Agee sidles around what he calls the soul: that which, he insists, can never be articulated or understood. His language seeks to "globe around" the unfathomable in order to evoke a sense that every person is a "center, soul, nerve" that is "globed around, with what shall make and harm him" (105).

"Two Images," a segment that Agee insists is "not words" but "only descriptions," epitomizes Book II's reverential treatment of the tenants. Iconic images of "Squinchy Gudger," the "Madonna's son," and of "Ellen Woods" curled up in sleep prompt a poetic explanation about "this center and source, for which we have never contrived any worthy name" (442). The description of these two images unfolds into a cultural prayer opening with the words of the title: "Let us now praise famous men." Befitting Agee's insistence on *human* divinity, this is a prayer not *to* God but *to* the "famous" of humanity—to the remembered ones, who led others peaceably, who "found out musical tunes, and recited verses in writing"; and to those "which have no memorial," the merciful, "whose righteousness hath not been forgotten" (445).

Human immortality, as Agee describes it, spirals forth as the unvanquishable repetition of the cycles of life and death. It is "as if flame were breathed forth from it and subtly played about it: and here in this breathing and play of flame, a thing so strong, so valiant, so unvanquishable, it is without effort, without emotion, I know it shall at length outshine the sun" (442). The sheer, obstinate persistence of the tenant families—the making of their own history in the face of a destitution not of their own making—enables us to "hope better of our children, and of our children's children" (439). As long as such testimonies to human divinity can be found, there is hope that with "their seed shall continually remain a good inheritance," an inheritance that helps human beings struggle to undo their social, economic, and intellectual shackles (445). Thus, the idea of human divinity contains the contradictory conditions of existence portrayed in *Let Us*. Coexisting with people's prescribed and imprisoned lives is the possibility of self-determination and freedom.

*H*uman divinity, as suggested in the syntactical progressions and revisioned images of Agee's descriptions, summons up and redefines an aesthetic of the sublime and the beautiful. In Agee's work, the sublime is the unrepresentable element of human existence, the excess he calls "human 'soul' " and the endlessness of human generations. Beauty, too, is intrinsic to existence, whether animate or inanimate. But the representation of anything—beautiful or otherwise—is a description, and " 'description,' " Agee states emphatically, "is a word to suspect" (238). Particularly suspect are those forms of description that claim to be objective, total, and universal, whether they derive from the domains of art, science, religion, philosophy, or politics. However, as Agee indicates, suspicion does not logically force one into silence but, rather, into modes of representation that openly defend one's interests, interpretations, and partialities.

Throughout the written text of *Let Us,* Agee uses the devices of music and film—forms of representation that he suggests emulate the reverberation and incessancy of life—as means of problematizing univocal representation. He announces in the preface that the work was written to be read aloud, because "variations of tone, pace, shape, and dynamics are here particularly unavailable to the eye alone, and with their loss, a good deal of meaning escapes" (xv). "It was also intended," he continues, "that the text be read continuously *as music is listened to or a film watched"* (xv; emphasis mine). In "(ON THE PORCH: 2," he states that music and film inform the work's structure. The book "as a whole," he writes, "will have a form and set of tones rather less like those of narrative than those of music," and he repeats in a footnote that the "forms of this text are chiefly those of music, of motion pictures, and of improvisations and recordings of states of emotion, and of belief" (244). He argues that traditional narrative produces a falsifying coherence of experience and clarity of time and space, whereas film and music come closer to the truth with "fragmentary renderings of some of the salient aspects of a real experience seen and remembered in its own terms"(246).

This valuation of music and motion pictures over traditional literary narrative reinforces Evans's privileging of the visual over the printed word. Time and time again, Agee calls attention to the inadequacies and inaccuracies of language. It is important to note, however, that he does not reject words but, instead, uses them to come as close as possible to what he calls an "illusion of embodiment." The writer who approximates such an illusion, he asserts, "accepts a falsehood but makes, of a sort in any case, better art" (238). By drawing on music and film to challenge the authority of the printed text, Agee casts doubt on any fixed relationship between word and thing while, at the same time, he strives for an embodiment, a "language of 'reality' " (236).

Agee notes that it is a "law of language" for "cow words [to try] to be a horse" (to try to create an illusion of univocal meaning) but adds that words are not to be unduly blamed for this, for the responsibility for word-use is the user's. He writes that the "cleansing and rectification of language, the breakdown of the identification of word and object, is very important, and very possibly more important things will come of it than have ever come of the lingual desire of the cow for the horse: but it is nevertheless another matter whenever words start functioning in the command of the ancient cow-horse law" (237). Given the "cow-horse law," by which words masquerade as objective descriptions of reality, Agee argues that it is necessary continually to disrupt that law by using words to create, instead, an "illusion of embodiment." In *Let Us,* Agee stages such a disruption by exposing his own consciousness at work as he makes truth-claims about himself and the tenants.

The placing of the writer's consciousness in the foreground of the work is not unique to Agee; it characterizes many modernist texts of his period. What is of particular interest here is the way in which Agee uses this literary technique to rethink the relationship between selfhood, representation, and truth in an aesthetics of liberty. His practice of self-stylization problematizes his own thought, his own assumptions, and his own modes of comprehension. He argues that, in order to get his "own sort of truth out of the experience," he handles it from "four planes":

> That of recall; of reception, contemplation, *in media res:* for which I have set up this silence under darkness on this front porch as a sort of fore-stage to which from time to time the action may have occasion to turn.
>
> "As it happened": the straight narrative at the prow as from the first to last day it cut unknown water.
>
> By recall and memory from the present: which is a part of the experience: and this includes imagination, which in the other planes I swear myself against.
>
> As I try to write it: problems of recording; which, too, are an organic part of the experience as a whole. (243)

Noting that these four planes are, "obviously, in strong conflict," he adds that so, too, is "any piece of human experience" (243).[7]

Although Agee's text has been criticized for its straining reminders of his presence as the orchestrating consciousness, for him, it is only through such a display of self-reflectivity that he can gain license to describe the tenants' lives and even his own experiences. Without such reminders, his descriptions would enter the discursive domain of the cow-horse law, a domain he challenges from the outset as both an impossibility and a fraud. By acknowledging the inherent limitations of his (and anyone's) discourse, he frees himself to apply linguistic vigor to embody, through musical and film-like "renderings," his truths of the tenants' existence.

Under the general heading "Some Findings and Comments," Agee divides his descriptions into five subheadings: Money, Shelter, Clothing, Education, and Work. These categories focus on the economic, spatial, physical, and disciplinary mechanisms that constitute the subjectivity of tenantry. In each case, Agee describes with genealogical specificity the ways in which the tenant families are subjected to power/knowledge mechanisms that confine them physically, mentally, emotionally, and imaginatively in dependency and poverty. This counterespionage data refuses to follow the conventions of social-science discourse. Instead, Agee locates himself as the partisan observer—the camera I/eye—who strives to impart empathetically everyday existence of the three families. The abundance of details—about planting, wages, debts, soil, floorboards, beds, jelly glasses, trousers, hats, shoes—forces reader-recognition of the activities of these individuals in making their own lives meaningful within and against social and economic determinants.

Here, as in other writings in America's tradition of an aesthetics of liberty, education represents a crucial set of power relations. Agee's unsparing critique of the school system is particularly noteworthy for the ways it redresses the discriminations based on class, race, and gender that characterize Jefferson's proposals for public education. At the same time, Agee renews the questioning and self-scrutiny characteristic of Jefferson's aesthetics of liberty. I quote the following lengthy passage not as a manifesto of education according to an aesthetics of liberty (which would be a contradiction in terms) but, rather, to show how Agee problematizes the normalizing and intellectually stunting curriculum he finds in the public schools, not just in Alabama but nationally. There is, he writes,

no setting before the students of "economic" or "social" or "political" "facts" and of their situation within these "facts," no attempt made to clarify or even slightly to relieve the situation between the white and negro races, far less to explain the sources, no attempt to clarify psychological situations in the individual, in his family, or in the world, no attempt to get beneath and to revise those "ethical" and "social" pressures and beliefs in which even a young child is trapped, no attempt, beyond the most nominal, to interest a child in using or in discovering his senses and judgment, no attempt to counteract the paralytic quality inherent in "authority," no attempt beyond the most nominal and stifling to awaken, to protect, or to "guide" the sense of investigation, the sense of joy, the sense of beauty, no attempt to clarify spoken and written words whose power of deceit even at the simplest is vertiginous, no attempt, or very little, and ill taught, to teach even the earliest techniques of improvement in occupation ("scientific farming," diet and cooking, skilled trades), nor to "teach" a child in terms of his environment, no attempt, beyond the most suffocated, to awaken a student either to "religion" or "irreligion," no attempt to develop in him either "skepticism" or "faith," nor "wonder," nor mental "honesty" nor mental "courage," nor any understanding of or delicateness in "the emotions" and in any of the uses and pleasures of the body save the athletic; no attempt either to relieve him of fear and of poison in sex or to release in him a free beginning of pleasure in it, nor to open within him the illimitable potentials of grief, of danger, and of goodness in sex and in sexual love, nor to give him the beginnings

at [the] very least of a knowledge, and of an attitude, whereby he
may hope to guard and increase himself and those whom he
touches, no indication of the damages which society, money, law,
fear and quick belief have set upon these matters and upon all
things in human life, nor of their causes, nor of their alternate
ignorances or possibilities of ruin or joy, no fear of doubtlessness,
no fear of the illusions of knowledge, no fear of compromise . . .
(292–93)

Thus, Agee turns the analytical categories of the human sciences
against themselves, showing not only how such classifications of
human existence exert a network of power constitutive of docile
subjectivity but also how the socioeconomic practices that operate in concert with those classifications perpetuate hierarchies
based on class, race, and gender. The need for persistent critique
of national and local pedagogy is one of the central premises of
an aesthetics of liberty.

After the five discussions in "Some Findings and Comments,"
and in keeping with Agee's request that we read the text as we
would watch a film, the next section is called "Intermission:
Conversation in the Lobby." With this "conversation," which includes an angry response to a questionnaire for American writers
circulated by *Partisan Review,* Agee addresses the intersections of
art, ethics, and politics. What has prompted his wrath at the editors of *Partisan Review* is the way their questionnaire presumes
the separateness of these spheres. Such a separation supports the
professionalization of the humanities and social sciences, segre-
gating and normalizing them. But disciplinary divisions may be
disrupted, like the naturalized narrative of film, by an intermission—a Brechtian alienation device that allows members of an
audience to take stock of their responses and communicate them
to each other. The intermission provides readers with a textual
lobby, a break for conversation about the representation of the
tenants and the aesthetic–ethical–political implications of that
representation.

Agee also draws on music to problematize univocal, authori-
tative meaning. With playfully serious irony, he reproduces a

short newspaper article in the "Notes and Appendices," intimating the role music might play in fostering freedom:

> BEETHOVEN SONATA
> HELD NO DISTURBANCE
> San Francisco, Dec. 6 (A.P.).—"Bee-
> thoven," said Judge Herbert Kaufman,
> "cannot disturb the peace."
> So he freed Rudolph Ramat, 69 years old
> and blind, of a charge of disturbing the
> peace by playing his accordion on Market
> Street.
> "Your honor," Ramat pleaded yesterday,
> "I have worked."
> —from the New York *Sun* (449–50)

He thus recontextualizes the prosaic newspaper-column format, treating the article as a poem or song in order to challenge the authority of both the law and the newspaper. And in keeping with his view of music as a guide to ethics, he uses Ramat's case to show that, while music might not "disturb the peace," it can disturb the workings of capitalism.

Agee's resourceful choice of music as a guide to truth reorients America's aesthetics of liberty for an age given to oscillating between claims of absolute certainty and absolute uncertainty, with corresponding tendencies toward domination and apathy.[8] Music, at once sensual, emotional, intellectual, and imaginative, confirms the value of all of these ways of knowing and experiencing. With it, Agee challenges the segregation of knowledge and experience by gender and race (women and blacks as sensual and emotional, white men as intellectual and artistic) and by discipline (science as unemotional and intellectual, art as sensory, emotional, and imaginative). Music tends to resist limitation: it is bounded and boundless, unique and iterable, consonant and dissonant, culturally specific and transculturally communicable. It is not, as Agee sometimes naively implies, inherently liberated or liberating, for it has been used in the service of totalizing systems of power (as has film). But in Agee's text it is used to assault totalitarian power on behalf of democratic freedom.

The three segments of "ON THE PORCH" demonstrate the importance of music to Agee's aesthetic ethics. They enact the interrelated autonomy of themes in a musical composition, suggesting also the way such themes are synchronized with each other and evolve through time. In these segments, meaning, like music, is changeable. Thematically, "ON THE PORCH" moves from silence to the paradoxical synchrony of silence with the undifferentiated sound out of which music is created. As the first segment opens, the "house and all that was in it" are "formal under the order of entire silence" (19). This "human silence," Agee writes, "obtained, prevailed, only locally, shallowly, and with the childlike and frugal dignity of a coal-oil lamp stood out on a wide night meadow and of a star sustained, unraveling in one rivery sigh its irremediable vitality, in the alien size of space" (20). Here, silence functions like the colon or the open-ended parenthesis of the title: the indeterminate and the prospective are poised beside that which has already been determined. The passage is consonant with Agee's view that individuals need to learn the art of silence.

"(ON THE PORCH: 2" fills in some of the space beyond the initial silence. In this section Agee states explicitly that the work has the form of music. He also links music with existence, first by describing how the "syncopations of chance" create a symmetry in life that is "in fact asymmetrical" (230) and, second, by discussing how that asymmetry "now seems to us to extend itself into a worrying even of the rigid dances of atoms and of galaxies" (231). This "hearing and seeing of a complex music in every effect and in causes of every effect and in the effects of which this effect will be part cause, and the more than reasonable suspicion that there is at all times further music involved there," he admits, " 'gets' us perhaps nowhere. One reason it gets us nowhere is that in a very small degree, yet an absolute one so far as each of us is capable, we are already there" (231). My reading of this rather ambiguous passage is that those who want to "get" somewhere fail to realize that they are "already there" because they harbor the deleterious illusion of a simplistic cause and effect, the view of life as a linear progression.

The last line of "(ON THE PORCH: 2" anticipates the music of the third segment by reporting that "a good way out along the hill there now came a sound that was new to us" (253). "(ON THE PORCH: 3" begins a discussion of the new sound by returning to the theme of silence with which the work opens. That initial silence, Agee states, "had stiffened us into much more intense silence," making both him and his companion, Walker Evans, "all one hollowed and listening ear" (463). The initial, "entire silence" thus becomes, in the third section, human responsiveness to an immersion in "noises that were all one noise" (463). The noise represents the multiplicity of existence, a multiplicity that can be differentiated into an infinite variety of meanings. These meanings are truthful, but they cannot capture the truth of the noise, which is undifferentiated sound. And it is only through relative silence surrounding individual voices that they can be differentiated from the "one noise." As Agee describes it, the night's blend of silent human listening and undifferentiated sound is suddenly pierced by the music of two animals calling to each other. "By use only of silences," the animal calls become a song of many meanings:

> One time it would be sexual; another, just a casual colloquy; another, a challenge; another, a signal or warning; another, a comment on us; another, some simple and desperate effort at mutual location; another, most intense and masterful irony; another, laughter; another, triumph; another, a masterpiece of parody of any one, any combination, or all of these assigned or implicit tones: but at all times it was beyond even the illusions of full apprehension, and was noble, frightening and distinguished: a work of great, private and unambitious art which was irrelevant to audience. (466)

The animal calls were "as perfect a piece of dramatic or musical structure as I know of," Agee comments, then tells how he and

Evans joined in the night's song by breaking into deep laughter (467). The dialogical character of the animal calls and this shared laughter—this music they create together—enacts the self-and-other relationship integral to Agee and Evans's aesthetics of liberty. Agee reports that once the animal calls subsided, he and Evans talked a bit and then drifted into their own thoughts, in a form of silence to the other but dialogue with the self. Finally, with the last words of the book, Agee depicts himself as provisionally accepting silence, when "at length we too fell asleep."[9] Their sleep punctuates the flux of undifferentiated existence just as silence turns incessant noise into meaning*ful*—but not necessarily harmonious—music.[10]

The final words of *Let Us* direct readers back to the beginning of the work and to the experiences that Agee states he "shall now try to give" (471). Guided by that suggestion, I now return to the opening pages of the written text in order to discuss what Agee identifies there as the two themes of the volume. I also note the limitations of the text as an attempt at counterespionage against normalizing power/knowledge. Here, two quoted passages bring together the photographic and written texts. The first is from *King Lear:*

> Poor naked wretches, wheresoe'er you are,
> That bide the pelting of this pitiless storm,
> How shall your houseless heads and unfed sides,
> Your loop'd and window'd raggedness, defend you
> From seasons such as these? O! I have ta'en
> Too little care of this! Take physick, pomp;
> Expose thyself to feel what wretches feel,
> That thou may'st shake the superflux to them,
> And show the heavens more just.

The second passage, which Agee has slightly altered, is from Marx and Engels:

> Workers of the world, unite and fight. You have
> nothing to lose but your chains, and a world to win.

A note following the second quotation says, "These words are quoted here to mislead those who will be misled by them. They mean, not what the reader may care to think they mean, but what they say. They are not dealt with directly in this volume; but it is essential that they be used here, for in the pattern of the work as a whole, they are, in the sonata form, the second theme; the poetry facing them is the first."

To argue that these words mean "what they say" is less a turn toward absolute meaning than it is an attack on whoever would limit the meanings of the passage by the univocal maneuver of dismissing it as communist party dogma. Agee concludes his note in a Jeffersonian vein: "In view of the average reader's tendency to label, and of topical dangers which any man, whether honest, or intelligent, or subtle, is at present liable, it may be well to make the explicit statement that neither these words nor the authors are the property of any political party, faith, or faction." (Jefferson once wrote: "I never submitted the whole of my opinions to the creed of any party of men whatever in religion, in philosophy, in politics, or in any thing else where I was capable of thinking for myself. Such an addiction is the last degradation of a free and moral agent. If I could not go to heaven but with a party, I would not go there at all" [letter to Francis Hopkinson, Mar. 13, 1779].)

Agee does not elaborate beyond insisting that the passages mean what they say, perhaps because he wants readers to inquire about their significance. My own thoughts are that the poetry and politics of the two passages converge to create a provisional space in which a subjectivity consonant with an aesthetics of liberty might take form. Lear asks: How shall the impoverished survive the "pitiless storm"? Answers lie in two directions, one poetic (the "I" and "thou" of the Lear passage) and the other political (the workers of the world). With "I have ta'en/Too little care of this!" Agee as author-narrator establishes identity with the formerly arrogant but now repentant Lear. The first-person narratives of *Let Us* depict an autobiographical process of coming into awareness and compassion, a struggle of the "I" to become an "eye" that sees the homelessness, hunger, and raggedness of the poor. The "you" of the poetry points to the tenants, and the "thou" addressed in "Take physick, pomp" extends generally to the privileged, who must learn to "feel what wretches feel." The text aims to encourage that learning of awareness and empathy, but as the second passage suggests, benevolence by those who enjoy the "superflux" is inadequate. The workers of the world must fight for greater justice.

These two passages encapsulate the book's attempt at counterespionage against normalizing power/knowledge and its use of poetic and musical forms to praise "human divinity" and to promote a social, political, and economic mission. But *Let Us* does not, and perhaps cannot as conceived, challenge certain fundamental hegemonic formations of power/knowledge. Despite its astute and bold assaults on univocal meaning and its evocation of the dignity of the tenants, it retains a self-other hierarchy. In short, its goal of empathy too often works against its goal of empowering people to fight on their own behalf. In the effort to empathize with the tenants—rather than to learn from them and work with them—the text suggests that Agee and Evans can speak for the tenants better than the tenants can speak for themselves: their counterespionage stops short of creating a forum for the tenants. This predicament of complicity in exploitation emerges in what Robert MacLean has called the work's "central anxiety" of voyeurism (33).[11] In Agee's prose, in particular, this anxiety is voiced in a confessional mode. His confessions themselves, by entangling him in ever-more-detailed self-analysis, repeat the very sins for which he seeks to be absolved.

But *Let Us* is not exclusively or even predominantly a work of agonizing moralists. It is, more importantly, the work of two men who, *as cultural workers,* combat the power/knowledge formations that normalize, classify, and discipline *them* as agents of surveillance. And their aesthetic-ethical stance—their bold opposition to the objectification of the other—constitutes their own practice of freedom. Read in this light, *Let Us* records the ways in which knowledge committed to the liberty of the other transforms the self. Without such self-stylization to ground the practice of freedom, the gathering of knowledge fosters objectification of both self and other.

Of the many vital contributions Agee and Evans make to America's aesthetics of liberty, their forging of a self-and-other ethos surely ranks among the most significant. Through the record of their personal coming-into-recognition of the tenants as individuals, they make visible the subjection of human beings by the dominant power/knowledge formations of American society. The first person of the text becomes a "we" ready to "challenge the fiend" of inhumane subjection. And in their reaccentuations of sublimity and beauty for an aesthetics of liberty, they refute the conceptualization of sublimity as controllable power and of beauty as homogeneous and universal. This is particularly important because they wrote and photographed during a period in which the sublime was used to inspire awe for fascist power, and discipline and beauty to conceal its grotesqueries.

CHAPTER FIVE

The Decentered Subject of Freedom: Kingston's *The Woman Warrior* and the Technology of Ideographic Selfhood

*I*n his 1982 essay entitled "The Subject and Power," Foucault argues that the modern era places individuals in a "kind of political 'double-bind,' which is the simultaneous individualization and totalization of modern power structures." He further suggests that "maybe the target nowadays is not to discover what we are but to refuse what we are," adding that, since this is the case, "we have to promote new forms of subjectivity through the refusal of this kind of individuality which has been imposed on us for several centuries" (424). I do not know whether Foucault was familiar with Maxine Hong Kingston's *The Woman Warrior*, published six years earlier. But it seems that Kingston, in the words she used to describe her childhood dream of becoming a warrior woman, anticipated that "the call would come" (20). In *The Woman Warrior* she promotes "new forms of subjectivity" by refusing the totalized, individualized subjectivity modern power structures produce.

Kingston's refusal includes rejection of the forms of representation that have promoted that subjectivity. The subtitle of *The Woman Warrior* specifies its genre: *Memoirs of a Girlhood Among Ghosts*. Kingston emphasizes the importance of her genre choice in an essay called "Cultural Mis-readings by American Reviewers," in which she states that she is "not writing history or sociology but a 'memoir' like Proust." She writes approvingly of two reviewers who recognize this point, stating that she is, "as Diane Johnson says, 'slyly writing a memoir, a form which . . . can neither [be] dismiss[ed] as fiction nor quarrel[ed] with as fact,'" and confirming Christine Cook's comment that "'the structure is a grouping of memoirs. . . . It is by definition a series of stories or anecdotes to illuminate the times rather than be autobiographical'" (64).

Despite these efforts at clarification, critics have continued to ignore or resist the implications of Kingston's work considered as memoirs. Paul John Eakins and Sidonie Smith show with insight and eloquence that the book challenges distinctions between fact and fiction, and they convert the *autos* or self of autobiography into a "self" understood either as self-invention (Eakin) or self-representation (Smith). But their readings of the work *as an autobiography*—even a postmodern one—underestimate its full-scale assault on modern power structures.[1]

Autobiography is a field of self-representation that historically has promoted the normalizing and disciplinary form of subjectivity that, as Foucault points out, we should "target." By contrast, the five memoirs of *The Woman Warrior* subject modern power formations to scrutiny by one who has been subjected to them.[2] *The Woman Warrior*'s aesthetics of liberty constructs a new form of subjectivity, what I call an *ideographic selfhood*: an ethical self-stylization that refuses the particular forms of selfhood, knowledge, and artistry that modern systems of power have made dominant. Practices of ideographic selfhood decenter normalized subjectivity by constructing an "I" that is itself a source of problemization of "what we are."

In the question whether to read *The Woman Warrior* as memoirs or as autobiography, more is at stake than the redressing of erroneous aesthetic assumptions about genre. At issue are the particular formations of subjectivity constructed by these different modes of discourse and by the technologies of power within which they operate. The modern memoir as a genre emerged more than two centuries before modern autobiography. (The

OED dates the first appearance of "memoir" in 1567 and that of "memoirs" in 1659. "Autobiography" makes its first appearance in 1809.) But as James M. Cox has argued, the term *autobiography* is now "so dominant that it is used retroactively to include as well as to entitle books from the present all the way back into the ancient world" (124).[3] This expansion of the term as a critical designation is a form of discursive colonization that produces and is produced by the dominant normalizing subjectivity of the post-Enlightenment West.

It is because of the differences between the ways the two genres typically constitute an "I" that autobiography has become established as a privileged aesthetic and ethical form of discourse in the modern era while memoirs retain a marginalized status. Autobiography promotes an "I" that shares with confessional discourse an assumed interiority and an ethical mandate to examine that interiority; memoirs promote an "I" that is implicitly constituted in reports of the utterances and proceedings of others. The "I" or subjectivity produced in memoirs is externalized and, in the Bakhtinian sense, overtly dialogical.[4] Unlike the subjectivity of autobiography, which is presumed to be unitary and continuous over time, memoirs (particularly in their collective form) construct a subjectivity that is multiple and discontinuous. The way an "I" is inscribed in memoirs therefore resists the modern era's dictum of individualized selfhood: Above all else, know thy interior self. In relation to autobiography, memoirs function as countermemory.

In situating autobiography as a self-normalizing practice of the modern era, it is important to recognize that autobiographies by marginalized people often have challenged the conventions and power relations of traditional autobiography, as can be seen in recent feminist scholarship such as Sidonie Smith's and in essay collections like *The Private Self* and *Life/Lines*.[5] If I make too harsh a case against autobiography, it is certainly not to dismiss those writings but to urge scrutiny of the extent to which they nevertheless promote the dominant subjectivity—the totalized individuality—of the modern era.[6] Furthermore, to label as "autobiographical" all types of life-writings—even when their titles announce them as memoirs, testimonials, confessions, and so on—tends to narrow our readings of them.[7] Memoirs may, of course, be used to promote reprehensible political programs, but they are a less effective means of doing so, given their marginalized status in the modern era and their dialogical format, which destabilizes unified selfhood.

Memoirs reject the discursive unity that constructs subjectivity as simultaneously individualized and totalized, for as the *OED* indicates, *memoirs* are composites of several types of discourse. The *OED* defines "memoir" as a "note, memorandum; record" and gives several definitions for plural "memoirs": "a record of events, not purporting to be a complete history, but treating of such matters as come within the personal knowledge of the writer, or are obtained from certain particular sources of information"; "a person's written account of records in his [sic] own life, of the persons whom he has known, and the transactions or movements in which he has been concerned; an autobiographical record"; "a biography, or biographical notice"; "an essay or dissertation on a learned subject on which the writer has made particular observations. Hence *pl.* the record of the proceedings or transactions of a learned society"; and finally, "a memento, memorial." *The Woman Warrior* is precisely such a composite.

The etymology of *memoirs* is particularly resonant for characterizing *The Woman Warrior.* Again from the *OED*: "F. *mémoire* masc., a specialized use, with alteration of gender, of *mémoire,* fem., MEMORY. The change of gender is commonly accounted for by the supposition that the use of the word in this sense is elliptical for *écrit pour mémoire;* Sp. Pg. and It. have *memoria* fem. in all senses." English usage retains a quasi-French pronunciation but has anglicized the spelling, making the word, according to the *OED,* "somewhat anomalous." Thus the word itself may be understood as a metonym for Kingston's discursive position. As a Chinese-American, she inherits two language systems, one with marginalized status. As a woman, she is a "somewhat anomalous" memoirist, using an etymologically feminine term that has been colonized by a masculine form. Thus, Kingston's subtitle signifies a subjugated femininity erupting against its linguistic and literary exclusion.

While Kingston uses the term *memoirs* in her subtitle as a generic description, she also uses the word *ghosts* to indicate that memoirs are not an exclusively empirical record of events and individuals. This places her in the lineage of Virginia Woolf, who, as Shari Benstock points out, also associates memoir writing with descriptions of "invisible presences." In *Moments of Being,* which includes five pieces Benstock calls "fragments of a memoir," Woolf describes the importance of these "invisible presences": "This influence, by which I mean the consciousness of other groups impinging upon ourselves; public opinion; what other people say and think; all those magnets which attract us this way to be like that, or repel us the other and make us different from that; has never been analyzed in any of those Lives which I so much enjoy reading, or very superficially" (quoted in Benstock 26). Benstock explains that Woolf's mother is one of these "invisible presences," not because she is absent from the memoir but rather because she is so much present: "too central, too close, to be observed" (Benstock 27). Woolf argues that "if we cannot analyze these invisible presences, we know very little of *the subject of the memoir*" (quoted in Benstock 27; emphasis mine).

In *The Woman Warrior,* ghosts have their own specificity as "invisible presences." Kingston represents her girlhood as triply displaced because of America's deeply embedded sinophobia, her parents' ambivalence about America given the poverty they face there, and the misogynistic attitudes she finds in both her American and Chinese heritages. The idea of ghosts suggests the profound confusion she felt as a child amidst the concealed but felt hatreds of both China and America. She is haunted by her mother's stories of women's oppression and female infanticide in China. She discloses her fear of those who performed the regular but often unseen services of quotidian life in America, which was, she says, "full of machines and ghosts—Taxi Ghosts, Bus

Ghosts, Police Ghosts, Fire Ghosts, Meter Reader Ghosts, Tree Trimming Ghosts, Five-and-Dime Ghosts" (96–97)—Americans who came regularly but without friendship, who filled the world with frightening noises and kept her family under surveillance. Both kinds of ghosts haunt her even into adulthood, but in adulthood the writing of her memoirs serves as a ritual of exorcism that "drives the fear away" (205). Thus, Kingston's memoirs confront what other forms of life-writing too often ignore—Woolf's pervasive "invisible presences," which are the most profound determinants of subjectivity.

The form of subjectivity explored in *The Woman Warrior* may be located at the nexus of the two patriarchal technologies of power, the deployment of alliance and the deployment of sexuality, which (as was discussed in the chapter on Fuller) interlock in the American nuclear family.[8] In *The Woman Warrior* the deployment of alliance—consisting of the "mechanisms of constraint" that operate through "a system of marriage, of fixation and development of kinship ties, of transmission of names and possessions" (*History of Sexuality* 106)—is associated with Kingston's Chinese heritage. In contrast, the deployment of sexuality is associated with American culture. Its mechanisms, as was indicated in the chapters on Thoreau and Fuller, operate not through legal constraint but by "proliferating, innovating, annexing, creating, and penetrating bodies in an increasingly detailed way, and controlling populations in an increasingly comprehensive way" (107). Within the family, the mother is a site of intersection between both systems.

Although, as Foucault demonstrates, the deployment of sexuality took shape from practices of alliance, particularly confession and penance, it now operates through the domains of medicine, education, police surveillance, and psychiatry. In regard to women in particular, one of the primary mechanisms of the deployment of sexuality is the process of "hysterization of women, which involve[s] a thorough medicalization of their bodies and their sex . . . carried out in the name of the responsibility they [owe] to the health of their children, the solidity of the family institution, and the safeguarding of society" (146–47). The mother's body is the site of integration (for herself and her children) into the medical sphere, and her fecundity is integrated into the social body through the "proper" production and moral education of children (104–6). Furthermore, in keeping with the dynamics of alliance, the mother perpetuates through her body the father's lineage, oversees the exchange of daughters in marriage, and maintains kinship ties.

Within the nuclear family, then, it is the mother's obligation to turn her daughter into a mother. To the extent that she succeeds, she aligns her daughter with herself at the point of intersection between the deployment of alliance and the deployment of sexuality. *The Woman Warrior* is a discourse of resistance to the subjectification of the daughter within this family dynamic. Such resistance is fraught with difficulties. Paramount among them is that, in trying to push away from the constraints of alliance's patriarchal law, daughters are pulled toward the enticements of sexuality's medicalizations. And a daughter's resistance carries with it the danger of severing her ties with her mother.

This dilemma is a paradigm of female subjectivity as it has been constituted in America. It is also an obstacle to the freedom of the subject. Insofar as a subject rejects patriarchal constraint by valorizing what Foucault has called "a hermeneutics of desire," she enters the domain of the deployment of sexuality; such a hermeneutics constructs subjects for whom the "truth of their being" is to be found in desire (including but not limited to sexual acts) (*Use of Pleasure* 5). On the other hand, insofar as a subject rejects the deployment of sexuality by valorizing essentialized womanhood and matriarchal kinship, she reverts to the system of alliance.

In this regard, *The Woman Warrior* is a particularly important text in the American ethical tradition of an aesthetics of liberty. Kingston situates the events of the book at the intersection within her family of the two systems of alliance and sexuality.[9] Through her depiction of her relationship to her mother, she portrays the dramatic intensity of mother-daughter relations within these interlocking power structures. In so doing, she demythologizes the ideal of the Mother and thus takes her problemization of motherhood a step beyond Fuller's essentialism. She combats both deployments of power by saying "no" to the repressions of patriarchal constraint without saying "yes" to the enticements of the sexualized body. At the same time, she forges a new kind of mother-daughter bond that does not require her to become yet another "dutiful daughter" in preparation for patriarchally circumscribed motherhood.[10]

Throughout *The Woman Warrior*, Kingston demonstrates how language, both oral and written, is one of the "invisible presences" constitutive of subjectivity.[11] The memoirs recount extensively Kingston's personal difficulties with language, focusing on them as a feature of the conflict of cultural impulses among Chinese-Americans generally and in her Chinese-American family specifically. As Sidonie Smith points out, Kingston suggests that her difficulty with language "originates in the memory of her mother's literally cutting the voice out of her" when she cut her frenum (Smith 168). In Kingston's words: "She pushed my tongue up and sliced the frenum. Or maybe she snipped it with a pair of nail scissors. I don't remember her doing it, only her telling me about it, but all during childhood I felt sorry for the baby whose mother waited with scissors or knife in hand for it to cry—and then, when its mouth was wide open like a baby bird's, cut" (163–64). The cut frenum serves as a figure for the dilemma of the conflicting subjectivities produced by the systems of alliance and sexuality, for the frenum is a membrane that both restrains and supports the tongue. "The Chinese," Kingston reports, "say 'a ready tongue is an evil'" (164). Yet her mother tells her that she cut her frenum in order to *give* her a ready tongue, telling her that her "tongue would be able to move in any language," that she would be "able to speak languages that are completely different from one another," a capacity she deems necessary for life in America (164). By the end of the text, this capacity is shown to be necessary in an interdependent world. But people who speak different languages are often derided in America, despite its multicultural citizenry; Jordan examines this issue as well.

Whatever her mother's motives, the predicament Kingston depicts as the result of the cutting is that of being caught between alliance's imposition of muteness on women and sexuality's pathology of hysterical babbling. Finding herself suspended in the spaces between Chinese and English, Kingston recounts that she fell into semi-muteness and experienced physical pain when required to speak aloud. After being cruel to another young girl, in many ways her double but one who has been less resistant to the imposed passivity of Chinese-American femininity, she experiences an eighteen-month-long "mysterious illness" in which she, like the "Victorian recluses [she] read about," remains indoors, a virtual invalid. Upon returning to school, she has "to figure out again how to talk" (182). But to talk is to risk becoming garrulously incoherent. Kingston cites examples of several women who are called insane, including her mother's sister, and fears that she, too, might lapse into mental illness. "Insane people," she observes, seemed to be "the ones who couldn't explain themselves" (186). In childhood her own self-explanations are so often blurred by the mix of two incommensurate languages that she feels not only unable to explain herself but unable even to understand the explanations of others. She finds consolation in talking to the "adventurous people inside [her] head" but fears that this is yet another sign of abnormality.[12]

From the adult perspective of the memoirs, Kingston indicates that these problems derived not so much from within her as from people's refusal to listen to those they deemed Other—those whose otherness they readily designated as abnormal. "A Song for a Barbarian Reed Pipe," the last of the five intertwining accounts that make up *The Woman Warrior,* relates a humiliating incident that crystallizes Kingston's sense of confused self as a child. Asked by her first-grade teacher to read a lesson aloud to the rest of the class, she faltered over the word "I." "I could not understand 'I,'" she recalls. The teacher, thoroughly enmeshed in the disciplinary pedagogical regime of the modern era, exiled her to a site of public shame—"the low corner under the stairs . . . where the noisy boys usually sat" (166–67).

The irony of course, is that the child had stumbled onto a profundity of which the teacher was unaware: the first person pronoun "I" is not at all simple; nor is it as unified as the "I" of autobiography implies. Kingston invites readers to see through her eyes as a Chinese-American child for whom writing had hitherto been ideographic. "The Chinese 'I' has seven strokes, intricacies. How could the American 'I,' assuredly wearing a hat like the Chinese, have only three strokes, the middle so straight?" (166). The child's question challenges the sense of self associated in Kingston's memoirs with nonideographic writing, a self that promises autonomy, certainty, and unequivocal moral rightness. The memoirs record that the phallic American "I" systematically denies its multiplicity and interconnectedness, masquerading as self-contained, independent subjectivity and imposing its will on others, often in the name of justice. The self-other dichotomy concealed within the American "I" stationed immigrant families in slums, then paved over the slums with parking lots; relegated immigrants to menial, low-paying labor; sneered at Chinese voices; used logic, science, and mathematics against "superstitious" modes of knowing; and branded children unable to read English with a "zero IQ" (48, 183).[13] Such an "I," Kingston warns, is not merely a harmful illusion; it is a form of imperialism.

Yet the alternative Chinese "I" is not without its own traps. Kingston points out that there is a "Chinese word for the female I—which is 'slave,'" adding with a note of bitterness that the Chinese "break the women with their own tongues!" (47). Thus, the ideographic conjunction of slave and female "I" represents the added problem confronting Kingston: her gender, which redoubles her second-class status as a Chinese-American. So pronounced is the legacy of female inferiority that it unsettles the love her family gives her. Even after she has left home as an adult, conflicting experiences of familial love and disdain haunt her. "From afar I can believe my family loves me fundamentally," she writes. "They only say, 'When fishing for treasures in the flood, be careful not to pull in girls,' because that is what one says about daughters." But rationalization fails in the face of nagging memories: "I had watched such words come out of my mother's and father's mouths; I looked at their ink drawing of poor people snagging their neighbors' flotage with long flood hooks and pushing the girl babies on down the river. And I had to get out of hating range" (52).

Kingston's "I" does not remain caught between an American facade of autonomy (belied for women, in any case, by the demands of what Kingston calls "American-feminine" behavior) and a Chinese sense of feminine inferiority. Rather, she challenges the operations of power in language, even at the level of writing as graphic inscription in the form of the Chinese ideograph and the American alphabet.[14] She rejects the notion that one can discover (invent or find) a language that "transcends" existing power formations. Instead, in *The Woman Warrior* she problematizes inherited intertwinings of writing, meaning, artistry, and experience and constructs a technology of the self that resists the subjectivities promoted by patriarchal ideographic and alphabetic language, using each tradition to challenge the other. She constructs a subjectivity through a form of writing that forces the American script of her text to reveal its intricacies in the way Chinese ideographs do.

The Woman Warrior, with its ideographic self, valorizes individual freedom while at the same time it defines selfhood as an ensemble subjectivity. The work disrupts Western conventions in this way and in terms of narrative time: the ideographic "I" mingles the distanced time of a retrospective point of view with the displayed time of processive narration.[15] This use of time opposes forms of historical and sociological discourse that promote the notion of objective reporting of events. Instead, like Agee with his four planes, Kingston displays the intersection of knowing subject and known object. The subjectivity that emerges from this conjunction is interdependent and interrelational, a self that acknowledges separation and difference from others while cultivating intimacy and interconnection. It is a subjectivity that recognizes the selfhood of the other and acknowledges its own alterity.[16] In short, Kingston's interventions in her inherited subjectivity constitute a technology of ideographic selfhood integral to an aesthetics of liberty.

As Foucault argues and as Kingston's critique of the Chinese and American "I" 's demonstrates, writing is a significant exercise of selfhood. Kingston challenges the ways that the deployment of alliance and the deployment of sexuality turn "real lives into writing," as Foucault says. *The Woman Warrior* rejects alliance's "procedure of heroization," which traditionally has chronicled the lives of powerful men—that is, men who have power over others. It relates, instead, stories about women who have been subordinated by such men. The memoirs also refuse the deployment of sexuality's "procedure of objectification and subjection," which disciplines and normalizes individuals in modern society (*Discipline and Punish* 192). Such "procedures" in writing construct subjectivities that either monumentalize individuals in the system of alliance or normalize them in the system of sexuality. Both forms of subjectivity deny or conceal the incoherencies, confusions, contradictions, and gaps constituting any selfhood. In opposition to claims for a unified and coherent subjectivity, Kingston accentuates the conflicts and confusions of identity that constitute her discursive "I." Her evocation of an ideographic selfhood acknowledges and creates a complex, discontinuous, multilayered subjectivity.

*K*ingston's technology of ideographic selfhood and its corresponding aesthetics and ethics entails putting into writing stories from the Chinese oral tradition, many of them told by her mother. Each story adds a stroke to Kingston's ideographic selfhood, and each stroke is a form of resistance to the deployments of power that would either constrain women's sexuality or hystericize it. The five titled accounts in *The Woman Warrior* display the operations of these power formations and of Kingston's opposition to them. The first two, the stories of No Name Woman and Fa Mu Lan, tell of the two women's limited attempts to counter the deployments of alliance and of sexuality. The third and fourth, representing the lives of Kingston's mother and aunt, reveal the detrimental effects of alliance and sexuality. And the final piece combines stories about the poetess Ts'ai Yen and Kingston's grandmother, who "loved the theater," to represent a subjectivity that emerges in resistance to both systems of power.

The first chapter of the memoirs, entitled "No Name Woman," retells a story told to Kingston by her mother on the occasion of the daughter's onset of menses. The mother tells of the plight of Kingston's father's sister, whose pregnancy by a man not her husband brands her a transgressor of village morality. No Name Woman refuses to identify the father of her child, thus giving her designation a double meaning—she has no name because she refuses to reveal his name. "She kept the man's name to herself throughout her labor and dying," Kingston writes. "She did not accuse him that he be punished with her. To save her inseminator's name she gave silent birth" (11). The patriarchal code of the deployment of alliance entitles the villagers to slaughter the family's animals, smear blood on their walls and doors, and yell curses at the pregnant woman. Facing a life of such ostracism for herself and her family, the aunt kills herself and her newborn baby by plunging into a well. This is a "spite suicide," Kingston notes, for it ruins the family's water supply. But drowning the baby with her is an act of love: "Mothers who love their children take them along" (15).

Over the years her aunt's drowned, "weeping" body with "wet hair hanging and skin bloated," seems always to wait "silently by the water to pull down a substitute" (16). In keeping with alliance's system of power, Kingston's mother tells her this story of family shame as a warning against sexual transgression, with a strict injunction never to tell of No Name Woman's existence, adultery, or suicide. Kingston not only tells her readers about her aunt, she embellishes the story with empathy. She also endows her aunt with a sexuality that her mother, as guardian of the villagers' sense of justice, would not tolerate. Twenty years after hearing about No Name Woman, Kingston refuses to continue in silent complicity with the code that exacted her death. By her public disclosure Kingston, too, transgresses the code of alliance and thus allies herself with her aunt. As Sidonie Smith argues, Kingston's "story thus functions as a sign, like her aunt's enlarging belly, publicizing the potentially disruptive force of female textuality and the matrilineal descent of texts" (156).

Kingston's revelation of the story of No Name Woman is her first act, in the memoirs, of self-empowerment through writing. It demarcates the nexus of alliance and sexuality within the family, a place where transgression within the system of alliance readily converts into the confessional mode of the system of sexuality.[17] *The Woman Warrior* allows us to see how feminist efforts to liberate women from the repressions of the patriarchal juridical code risk entrapping them more deeply in the deployment of sexuality's proliferating dynamics of power. More importantly, Kingston, like Thoreau, resists this pull through a strategy of desexualization, replacing the prescribed practices of morality, normality, and artistry with "other forms of pleasures, of relationships, coexistences, attachments, loves, intensities" ("Power and Sex" 116). "White Tigers," the second piece in the memoirs, represents a point of departure for this resistance against the power dynamics that otherwise would pull Kingston's sexual/textual transgression into the confessional mode. In this way she avoids one of the pitfalls of autobiography: its frequent complicity in the confessional mechanism of the deployment of sexuality.

It should be stressed that "White Tigers" is only a beginning. Its blending of self-sacrifice and justice is a child's fantasy of heroics, a fantasy that powerfully but *playfully* combines the figure of the legendary Fa Mu Lan with kung fu heroes from American movies.[18] As a child, Kingston learned a chant of her mother's about Fa Mu Lan, a woman warrior who had avenged her village and family for crimes committed by a cruel and aggressive baron. She became infatuated with Fa Mu Lan because, unlike the American and Chinese women Kingston knew, the warrior was honored for her deeds both in battle, from which women are traditionally excluded, and in patriarchal motherhood, through which women have been subordinated. Thus, imagination provided an outlet against the double devaluation Kingston had experienced as a Chinese-American girl. In the theater of her mind she became this woman warrior who underwent strenuous years of discipline and training in order to take her place as both soldier and mother. Ultimately, however, like No Name Woman, whose challenge to the system of alliance ended in defeat, Kingston manages only a partial challenge to the process of sexualization through her fantasies of being a female avenger.

Ideographs inaugurate the fantasy world of "White Tigers" and indicate the development of an ideographic selfhood. Initially, nature's ideographs summon the child to the challenge of greater humanity. "The call would come," Kingston writes, "from a bird that flew over our roof. In the brush drawings it looks like the ideograph for 'human,' two black wings" (20). When the call comes, the girl of seven leaves home to join an old man and old woman who train her to become a warrior. The training includes exercises resembling body writing: "I learned to move my fingers, hands, feet, head, and entire body in circles. I walked putting heel down first, toes pointing outward thirty to forty degrees, making the ideograph 'eight,' making the ideograph 'human.' . . . I could copy owls and bats, the words for 'bat' and 'blessing' homonyms" (23). After years of preparation, she returns home to bid her parents farewell before leaving for battle. The theme of inscription is repeated as her parents mark her body with their love and desire for revenge. By carving into her back their "oaths and names," they transform her body into a testament of family honor. "My father first brushed the words in ink," she records. "Then he began cutting; . . . My mother caught the blood and wiped the cuts with a cold towel soaked in wine. It hurt terribly—the cuts sharp; the air burning; the alcohol cold, then hot—pain so various. . . . If an enemy should flay me, the light would shine through my skin like lace" (34–35). In battle, the woman warrior avenges her family and village, regaining their lands; while still at war, she marries her childhood friend and bears a child. Finally, she returns victorious to her village to live out her days in honor.

The fantasy segment of "White Tigers," with its heroic deeds and "happily ever after" ending, is juxtaposed with a concluding section about real events from Kingston's life: her struggles to bring about gender, racial, and class equality and her attendant feelings of frustration, impotence, and confusion. Marching and studying at Berkeley in the sixties does not turn her into the boy her parents would have preferred. Confronting an employer with his racism, she is dismissed from her job. She tells the story of an uncle in China who was killed by the Communists for stealing food for his family rather than giving it to the "commune kitchen to be shared"; she finds it "confusing that my family was not the poor to be championed" (51). And she laments her inability to avenge her family: "I'd have to storm across China to take back our farm from the Communists; I'd have to rage across the United States to take back the laundry in New York and the one in California. Nobody in history has conquered and united both North America and Asia" (49).

Although the heroics of Fa Mu Lan are naive in terms of political practice, the story of the female avenger is a bold stroke in Kingston's creation of ideographic selfhood. Telling the story is an inverse expression of Kingston's powerlessness as a Chinese-American female, but an expression that ultimately empowers her as an author and allows her to become a different kind of warrior: one who makes public the wrongs suffered by her people. Comparing herself to the woman warrior of her fantasy, as in the title of the memoirs, she observes that what "we have in common are the words at our backs. The ideographs for *revenge* are 'report a crime' and 'report to five families.' The reporting is a vengeance—not the beheading, the gutting, but the words. And I have so many words—'chink' works and 'gook' words too—that they do not fit on my skin" (53). As a writer-warrior, then, Kingston uses the image of words *in excess* of her body to suggest that writing itself must veer away from monumentalizing and normalizing regimes of discourse and serve instead to corporealize a subjectivity that can take revenge on forces of domination. This excess of words disrupts racist and sexist categories of containment through which the dominant and dominating regimes of power in America are constructed.

Much of the drama of *The Woman Warrior* derives from Kingston's representation of her mother as a force of domination.[19] Rather than suppressing the ambivalence her mother inspires, Kingston evokes her powerful presence and painfully explores the difficulty of identifying with, yet separating from, her mother. This involves confrontation with the two systems of power that intersect within the family. The process is a precarious one that threatens to end in repudiation of the mother or abandonment by her—the two possibilities that terrified Kingston as a child. Yet to model herself after her mother would perpetuate two modes of oppression: the subordination of women within the deployment of alliance, and their hysterization within the deployment of sexuality. By writing her memoirs, Kingston alters this dynamic, separating herself from her mother without severing their ties.

Kingston does this by intertwining two discursive threads integral to her technology of ideographic selfhood: healing and artistry. But to create a new pattern, she must first unravel the designs of her double heritage: Chinese shamanism and the oral tradition of the mother, which maintained the deployment of alliance, and American science and medicine and the written tradition of the father, which maintained the deployment of sexuality. In *The Woman Warrior,* particularly in the third chapter, "Shaman," which she devotes to her mother, Brave Orchid, Kingston describes her mother's practices of midwifery and healing. Brave Orchid's shamanism seems to the child like magic in comparison to the science and logic she learns in school in order to become "American-normal." Although Kingston admires her mother and the other women of the To Keung School of Midwifery as "outside women"—"new women, scientists who changed the rituals"—she deems her mother's shamanistic practices to be superstitious and frightful. Such is the case, for example, with the "big brown hand with pointed claws stewing in alcohol and herbs," stored in a jar from which Brave Orchid draws "tobacco, leeks, and grasses" to apply to her children's wounds (91). So, too, with the power over life and death that her mother possessed as a midwife in China. Kingston sees that her mother's diploma is disparaged by American health agencies; as a result, Brave Orchid must labor long hours as a laundry worker and tomato picker instead of in the profession for which she was trained. "This is terrible ghost-country," she reports her mother saying, "where a human being works her life away" (104).

Although Kingston sympathizes with her mother's professional exclusion in America, she shares many of the American attitudes toward shamanism. These conflicting feelings are intensified when Brave Orchid's treatments prove ineffectual and possibly harmful to the mental health of her sister, Moon Orchid. The story of Moon Orchid's deterioration is the subject of the fourth memoir, "At the Western Palace." Brave Orchid's ministrations might well have worked in the sisters' Chinese village decades earlier, where alliance's system of knowledge and morality prevailed. But in America they lead to Moon Orchid's commitment to an insane asylum by Western medical authorities. To accept her mother's beliefs, Kingston implies, might invite such a judgment on her as well. She determines to differentiate herself from her mother through adherence to Western science and logic.

Yet the wish to be sane has an underside, as is illustrated by Moon Orchid's response to the mental asylum. There she finds happiness in the company of other women who "speak the same

language" (160). The combined dread of and longing for insanity
that Kingston expresses throughout *The Woman Warrior* results
from the deployment of sexuality's hysterization of women.
For to be a "proper" (procreative) woman within this technology means to be medicalized: it means becoming either the
"American-normal" Good Mother or the abnormal, hysterical
woman. In describing the eighteen-month illness of her childhood, when she lived "like the Victorian recluses," Kingston reveals the thrill of invalidation that is central to the invalidism of
hysteria: "It was the best year and a half of my life. Nothing
happened" (182). Such yearning for nothingness is a consequence
of overidentification with patriarchally inscribed motherhood: a
desire to return to prelinguistic infancy in order to evade the subjectivity that becoming a mother entails in the nexus of alliance
and sexuality. This yearning may be understood as a form of resistance to women's subordination in a misogynistic society, but
it is a paradoxical resistance that turns on itself, destroying not
misogyny but the woman who suffers it.

Instead of entering the sphere of hysterization, Kingston creates a self-healing aesthetics. This requires differentiation from
her mother's artistry, for, as with Brave Orchid's medicine, the
mother's art functions primarily within the system of alliance.
Throughout her childhood, her mother's talk-stories filled Kingston's imagination with "pictures to dream," some of them rev-
eries of hope, as with the legend of Fa Mu Lan, others
nightmarish, as with the story of No Name Woman and the
monkey story in which eaters feast on the brain of a still-living
monkey. Even though Brave Orchid is an artist, she remains
within her oral tradition, and her stories often are accompanied
by the admonition not to tell them to anyone. Thus, Kingston's
written memoirs are a sign of separation from her mother's oral
tradition and from the tradition of women's enforced silences.
But they are also a tribute to her mother: to the vividness of
her stories and to her readiness to confront some of life's greatest terrors.

Enthralled by the mother's courage, aware of her vulnerabil-
ity, and caught within her complicated and often hostile attitude

toward females, Kingston lives her childhood in the interstice between two cultures, a place where she is in danger of plunging into either "feminine" muteness or hysteria. Acquiring a new voice is an important feature of her self-stylization. However, she finds it through an over-zealous repudiation of her mother. One day as they work together in the family laundry, she blurts out angrily: "I won't let you turn me into a slave or wife. . . . They say I'm smart now. Things follow in lines at school. They take stories and teach us to turn them into essays. . . . And I don't want to listen to any more of your stories; they have no logic. They scramble me up. You lie with stories" (201–2). Although the memoirs suggest that such vehemence was crucial for constructing a new subjectivity, she follows this passage with a note of regret: "Be careful what you say. It comes true. It comes true. I had to leave home in order to see the world logically, logic the new way of seeing. I learned to think that mysteries are for explanation" (204). Acquisition of the deployment of sexuality's empirical knowledge displaces the system of alliance's shamanistic knowledge.

But the Western logic constitutive of Kingston's new subjectivity does not entirely supplant Brave Orchid's way of knowing: the memoirs use—and challenge—both. In *The Woman Warrior*, Kingston combines her mother's talk-stories with logical details that seek to explain without reducing complexities.[20] And in it she pays tribute to her mother as artist and healer even as she separates herself from her. In these ways, the memoirs show how one can symbolically revisit one's mother through writing, not as a child but as an adult, giving birth to oneself as an artist with the aid of the mother's midwifery.

Despite the difficulties in the relationship between Kingston and her mother because of their clashing views, that relationship ultimately provides the momentum for Kingston's new—but never complete, never closed—ideographic subjectivity. Kingston's memoirs refuse alignment with phallic conceptualizations of art that ignore the mother's role as a teacher of language, define the mother tongue as crude in relation to the fatherly text, or see artistry as a symbolic playing out of the Oedipal conflict between father and son. *The Woman Warrior* draws on Brave Orchid's talk-stories and shamanism even as it marks Kingston's turn toward a written art that exposes and questions them in order to heal the wounds of patriarchal motherhood and daughterhood.[21]

The story of Ts'ai Yen enacts this change of direction. It concludes the memoirs with a tribute to the power of a woman who transformed the sounds of captivity into piercingly beautiful music. Kingston writes that this is a "story my mother told me, not when I was young, but recently, when I told her I also am a story-talker. The beginning is hers, the ending, mine" (206). Her mother's story is about her own mother, Kingston's grandmother, who so loved the theater that she moved the entire family, as well as some of the household furnishings, to the theater when the actors came to her village. This was done to ensure the household's safety from bandits while the family was away enjoying the performance, but the bandits attacked the theater. They scattered the family and very nearly kidnapped Lovely Orchid, Kingston's youngest aunt. After the ordeal, however, "the entire family was home safe, proof to my grandmother that our family was immune to harm as long as they went to plays." She adds that "they went to many plays after that" (207).

The family's frequent attendance at the theater is both a logical non sequitur and a meaning-producing narrative thread between her mother's story and Kingston's. "I like to think that at some of those performances, they heard the songs of Ts'ai Yen," writes Kingston (207). This telling phrase, "I like to think," encapsulates the ethics, poetics, and politics of Kingston's aesthetics of liberty. As Trinh Minh-ha has observed, Kingston's writing, which is "neither fiction nor non-fiction, constantly invites the reader either to drift naturally from the realm of imagination to that of actuality or to live them both without ever being able to draw a clear line between them yet never losing sight of their differentiation" (135). Just as the village theater serves in her mother's story as the space of both fear and fortune, of cause and effect, so too, the phrase "I like to think" serves in Kingston's memoirs as the field of the represented and the not yet represented, the recalled and the imagined. And the ending of the tale demonstrates that what is representable—and what is not—can be altered.

Ts'ai Yen, a poet born in A.D. 175, was captured at the age of twenty by a barbarian tribe. By day over the twelve years of her captivity, she could hear only the "death sounds" of war, but at night the desert air was filled with the sharp, high notes of her captors' reed flutes. Fascinated by their disturbing music, she finally taught herself to sing "a song so high and clear, it matched the flutes": a song in her own language, in words her captors could not understand, but filled with a "sadness and anger" that they could not fail to comprehend. When she was later ransomed and returned home, she brought her songs with her. One of these songs is "Eighteen Stanzas for a Barbarian Reed Pipe," a song that Chinese now "sing to their own instruments" (206–9).

Perhaps like Ts'ai Yen's song, Kingston's memoirs sustain her in a hostile land. But unlike Ts'ai Yen, who eventually returns home, the hostile land from which Kingston writes *is* her homeland. Its endemic ethnic, gender, and class hatreds give rise to a sense of displacement akin to that evoked by her ambivalent relationship to her mother and inspire a corresponding yearning for place. Kingston rethinks women's place not only in regard to the family but also in regard to territoriality.[22] This issue arises during a visit to her parents' home when she is an adult. Seeing her mother's distress over having to relinquish the last of their land in China, she responds: "We belong to the planet now, Mama. Does it make sense to you that if we're no longer attached to one piece of land, we belong to the planet? Wherever we happen to be standing, why, that spot belongs to us as much as any other spot" (107). This remark consoles even as it refuses a mythologized evocation of an originary homeland.

Kingston's concept of belonging to the planet contrasts with the metaphor of perpetual exile proposed by Edward Said, Tzvetan Todorov and Julia Kristeva as an ethical guide. Both Said and Todorov quote Erich Auerbach (who, in turn, quotes

Hugh of St. Victor of the twelfth century): "The man who finds
his country sweet is only a raw beginner; the man for whom
each country is as his own is already strong; but the man for
whom the whole world is as a foreign country is perfect"
(Todorov 250). And Kristeva argues that exile "is an irreligious
act that cuts all ties, a severing necessary for thought" ("A New
Type of Intellectual" 298–99). *The Woman Warrior* suggests that
such a stance goes too far in denying the ties between individuals and their planet. To hold that one belongs to the planet, and
to claim as one's own the spot wherever one happens to be
standing, resists nation-state mythologies without mythologi-
zing exile.

C hinese-Americans, when you try to understand what things
in you are Chinese, how do you separate what is peculiar to
childhood, to poverty, insanities, one family, your mother who
marked your growing with stories, from what is Chinese? What
is Chinese tradition and what is the movies?" asks Kingston in
the opening pages of *The Woman Warrior* (5–6). Over the course
of her memoirs she indicates that she cannot, in fact, separate
what is peculiar to her own life and family from what is Chinese,
or even from the American version of what is Chinese. Indeed,
in the ethical aesthetics of the memoirs, experience is neither sep-
arable nor unmediated but is always a knot of significations. One
can, however, perhaps especially through the writing of one's
memoirs, give new meanings to the twists and ties of knotted
experience, new meanings that challenge those prescribed by hegemonic technologies of power and selfhood.

A metaphor of knot making opens the final memoir of *The
Woman Warrior*. Kingston contrasts her form of storytelling with
her brother's, which is notable for its barrenness; it is not
"twisted into designs" like hers. She points to the dangers of
such knot making but insists on its importance. "Long ago in
China," she writes, "knotmakers tied strings into buttons and
frogs, and rope into bell pulls. There was one knot so compli-

cated that it blinded the knotmaker. Finally an emperor outlawed this cruel knot, and the nobles could not order it anymore." "If I had lived in China," she adds, "I would have been an outlaw knotmaker" (163). In this vignette, as with her comparison between the American and Chinese "I" 's, Kingston uses a Chinese tradition to challenge American ones. Her representation of storytelling as knot making alludes to the ancient Chinese practice called *chien sheng,* or "knotted cord," a method for keeping records and communicating information (Carus 2–3).[23] By tying together her life experiences in a "cruel knot" of blinding truth, Kingston becomes an "outlaw knotmaker," a not-maker or negater of patriarchal law and normalizing power.

Just as the ideograph's several intersecting strokes display its polysemy, so too, the knot as a symbol of discursive form suggests the possibility of untying old meanings and retying new ones. Through such untying and retying, Kingston seeks to "figure out how the invisible world the emigrants built around our childhoods fit in solid America" (5). In this figuring-out, which is a figuring-*of* what is peculiar to her, Kingston calls in question the limits of her subjectivity. As Foucault observes "the critique of what we are is at one and the same time the historical analysis of the limits that are imposed on us and an experiment with the possibility of going beyond them" ("What is Enlightenment?" 50). *The Woman Warrior* presents ideographic self-stylization as a practice of going beyond imposed limits.

CHAPTER SIX

The "Astropotamous" Significance of Specific Intellectuals: Jordan's *On Call* and the Practice of Liberty

*I*n "Power and Sex," an interview given shortly after the publication of *History of Sexuality*, Foucault was asked whether he thought his work might fill the "gap" in contemporary theoretical discourses between the model of power as law or interdiction and the Marxist conceptualization of power as class struggle. He replied that he didn't "make any such claim" (123–24). This reply could be taken merely as a pose of humility. But it was far more significant. It was a criticism of the assumption inherent in the question, namely, that Foucault's theorizing about power came from a place outside power, the place presumed to be held by the universal intellectual. In a Foucauldian analytics of power/knowledge, no such place of "free" consciousness exists, for one always occupies a specific position traversed by multiple lines of power/knowledge. Arguing that the "prophetic function" of intellectuals was being, or at least should be, abandoned, he described what he hoped would replace the model of the "Greek wise man, the Jewish prophet, the Roman legislator":

> I dream of the intellectual who destroys evidence and generalities, the one who, in the inertias and constraints of the present time, locates and marks the weak points, the openings, the lines of force, who is incessantly on the move, doesn't know exactly where he is heading nor what he will think tomorrow for he is too attentive to the present; who, wherever he moves, contributes

to posing the question of knowing whether the revolution is worth the trouble, and what kind (I mean, what revolution and what trouble), it being understood that the question can be answered only by those who are willing to risk their lives to bring it about. ("Power and Sex" 124)

Thus, Foucault explained why he would not claim to have filled the "gap" between the juridically and class-based models of power, although he might well be credited with having created it. To claim to fill the gap would have implicated him in the two models of power he argued were inadequate in their exclusive focus on law and class. To speak as a universal intellectual would promote the workings of the proliferating mechanisms of normalizing bio-power that he had criticized so forcefully in *History of Sexuality*.[1]

Unlike the predictive and legislative intellectual who presumes to speak on behalf of others in the name of universal justice, the intellectual of Foucault's "dream" recognizes herself or himself (Foucault's use of the generic masculine pronoun notwithstanding) as struggling from within the power/knowledge formations of a given society. In "Truth and Power," he calls this kind of intellectual a "specific intellectual" (126) and explains what he sees as the relationship between the specific intellectual and power/knowledge:

> The essential political problem for the intellectual is not to criticise the ideological contents supposedly linked to science, or to ensure that his own scientific practice is accompanied by a correct ideology, but that of ascertaining the possibility of constituting a new politics of truth. The problem is not changing people's consciousness—or what's in their heads—but the political, economic, institutional regime of the production of truth.
>
> It's not a matter of emancipating truth from every system of power (which would be a chimera, for truth is already power) but of detaching the power of truth from the forms of hegemony, social, economic and cultural, within which it operates at the present time. (133)

The work of "constituting a new politics of truth" is a work of reconstituting power relations. Like the operations of normalizing power/knowledge, which are always on the move, establishing themselves in new lines of force, the specific intellectual must be on the move, finding new weak points to target, new fault lines upon which the edifices of the hegemonic regime of truth have been built.

The work of a specific intellectual is also the work of self-transformation. In another interview Foucault described his own efforts in a more personal and jocular vein:

> You see, that's why I really work like a dog and I worked like a dog all my life. I am not interested in the academic status of what I am doing because my problem is my own transformation. That's the reason also why, when people say, "Well, you thought this a few years ago and now you say something else," my answer is, *[Laughter]* "Well, do you think I have worked like that all those years to say the same thing and not be changed?" This transformation of one's self by one's own knowledge is, I think, something rather close to the aesthetic experience. Why should a painter work if he is not transformed by his own painting? ("The Minimalist Self" 14)

In short, the work of the specific intellectual is a practice of self-stylization.

June Jordan's work as a specific intellectual is just such a practice of self-transformation "by one's own knowledge." It is a strategic struggle against contemporary American normalizing bio-powers, which increasingly extend their fields of operation into other countries and reinforce the deployments already in place. Jordan's work is also a struggle against the continuing deployments of alliance, both in the patriarchal family and in American imperialistic interventions in postcolonial countries. The articles, letters, and lectures gathered together in *On Call* make vital contributions to America's ethics of an aesthetics of liberty. These essays participate in a "new politics of truth" by engaging in a "battle about the status of truth and the economic and political role it plays" ("Truth and Power" 132).

Writing as a black-woman-mother-daughter-poet-professor-political essayist, Jordan advances an aesthetic ethics that counters the tendency to universalize. Universalizing discourses, whether of the dominant order or of the radical Left, tend toward totalization: the eradication of heterogeneity.[2] They do so in tribute to human sameness. The idea that all individuals are essentially the same is still an appealing one to many. But in the context of normalizing bio-powers, notions of sameness are used to exclude, divide, and punish people who don't fit the categories of the universal—the categories that stipulate what is normal, acceptable, or correctable. In opposition to the universal and the coherent, Jordan's ethics employs heterogeneity as an aesthetic category. In her notion of subjectivity, homogeneity—the presumption of which is integral to a normalizing hermeneutics of desire—threatens the freedom of the subject.

The poststructuralist concept of the multiply-designated subject is relevant here. As Lauren Berlant argues, we might think of the "multiply-designated or affiliated subject [as] defined by his/her engagement with disparate and dissimilar discourses." She also points out that, while "the subject *in theory* might negotiate fully articulated relations with his/her multiple sites of affiliation, *in practice* the subject's critical task would be more humble: to identify relations of colonization, suppression, positive association, and so on, in an always provisional attempt to map out the dominant logic of identity" (255n.9). Jordan, with her appeals to heterogeneity, presents a similar view of the subject's engagement with multiple discourses. This subject, guided by categories of sublimity and beauty, is capable of aesthetic-ethical transformation or, as Jordan calls it, "self-determination" that is itself a practice of liberty.

The concept of a multiply-designated subjectivity emerges from postmodern cultural conditions. As cultural theorists on both the right and the left have pointed out, some features of late capitalism subject individuals to fragmentation rather than the homogenization produced by normalizing power relations. An ethical-aesthetic understanding and use of multiple designation (or ideographic selfhood) resists both late capitalism's production of fragmented subjectivity and normalizing technologies' constitution of homogenized, totalized subjectivity.

On Call consists of eighteen essays or chapters about complex, overlapping subjects, including Walt Whitman's poetry, Jordan's mother's suicide, her marriage to and divorce from a white man, and the oppression of blacks in South Africa. The introduction explains why these pieces, written between 1981 and 1985 and often topical in focus, are gathered together for publication in a book: the reason is American censorship. This censorship works in a variety of ways. One is formalized exclusion. "If you will count the number of Black women with regular and national forums for their political ideas, and the ideas of their constituency," she writes, "you will comprehend the politics of our exclusion: I cannot come up with the name of *one* Black woman in that position" (1). Without such a forum, writings such as Jordan's, if they are accepted for publication at all, are vulnerable to depoliticization, as when one of her essays on class and race was placed in the Travel and Leisure section of a leading women's magazine (2). Often, her writings have not been accepted; she quotes editors as explaining: "Many of us have problems with your position on Nicaragua. Or the Middle East" (3). In other words, within the domain of the American press, an opinion that is deemed too controversial is considered unworthy of a public forum. Such denial of diverse voices prohibits dialogue about difficult, complex issues and thus restricts practices of liberty. Jordan has managed, in part by gaining the credentials that white Americans have established as necessary for credibility— a degree from Barnard, international acclaim for her poetry, a professorship of English at SUNY Stonybrook—to get her position recognized.

South End Press has served as a non-mainstream forum for Jordan, from which to battle censorship and demand thought about the issues she addresses. So, even if we cannot read her writings concurrently with the events they analyze, we can, at least, read them. *On Call* is Jordan's second volume of political essays; the first volume, *Civil Wars,* is (as the biographical note on the author states) the "first such work to be published by a Black woman in the United States." Doubly marginalized by race and class, Jordan directly challenges the technology of normalizing media communication, refusing to be silenced.

By bringing together essays that ordinarily would appear as separate pieces, *On Call* encourages a reading of them as part of the tradition of an American ethics of an aesthetics of liberty. As separate works, they all promote an aesthetic ethics of individual and civic self-determination and argue against the disciplinary boundaries dividing art, politics, and ethics. In keeping with the view of writing as a way of reflecting on the self, each essay addresses some current truth and explores its presumptions, implications, and consequences for the "I" who writes. Gathering these pieces together in book form accentuates their role in the author's self-stylization as she engages in practices of problemization to produce a new politics of truth.[3]

Of particular significance are the ways in which the collection problematizes universalizing tendencies involving rights, justice, and equality. In *Notes,* Jefferson espouses universalized Enlightenment principles but also suggests the importance for each generation of rethinking the meaning of freedom. Such rethinking has been integral to subsequent writings promoting an aesthetics of liberty. By insisting on specificity in her discussions of rights, justice, and equality, Jordan continues Jefferson's work of problemization by thought. *On Call*'s discussions of the domains of bio-power (the family, medicine, schools, the police, the military) and their relationship to law expose oppressive modes of subjectivity. And in promoting the freedom of the subject, *On Call* sponsors a non-normalizing ethics of an aesthetics of liberty.

*O*n *Call* opens with a tribute to Walt Whitman as a writer of people's poetry and a celebrator of heterogeneity. Unlike the white fathers who established a republic sanctioning slavery, and unlike the white fathers who proclaim that poetry and politics are and must be distinct, and unlike a white father such as

Denis Donoghue, whose Eurocentric literary perspective "comfortably excluded every possible descendent of Whitman" (13), Whitman is a democratic "white father" of the New World. In this opening chapter, Jordan reinscribes the aesthetic categories of sublimity and beauty for a New-World ethics that opposes the Old-World values of hierarchy: "New World means non-European; it means new; it means big; it means heterogeneous; it means unknown; it means free; it means an end to feudalism, caste, privilege, and the violence of power. It means *wild* in the sense that a tree growing away from the earth enacts a wild event" (11). She places herself within a New World genealogy: "I too am a descendent of Walt Whitman" (14).

What has been the history of the descendents of Whitman in America? Jordan evokes the political sublime by commemorating "all of the poets whose lives have been baptized by witness to blood, by witness to cataclysmic, political confrontations, from the Civil War through the Civil Rights era, through the Women's Movement, and on and on through the conflicts between the hungry and the well-fed, the wasteful, the bullies" (14). This violence of struggle on battlefields and in the streets has its counterpart in struggles against the quieter violence of exclusion in the classrooms and in the canonical tradition of the American literary establishment. But the descendents of Whitman—in "Poets to come!" he calls them the "new brood, native, athletic, continental, greater than before known"—have fulfilled his expectation of "main things" from them; and as Jordan reminds her readers in closing; she and other New-World poets "go on singing this America" (15).

Even as Jordan places herself in an aesthetic-ethical-political lineage with Whitman, in a later chapter she antedates his New-World tradition in the *"difficult* miracle of Black poetry in America" and in the oppressive beginnings of that tradition (97). The genealogy of black American poetry begins in Africa, with a child whose African origins, name, and language remain unrecorded in American history. The child was taken from her home, sent across the ocean, placed on an auction block, bought by

Suzannah and John Wheatley, and given their surname and the designation Phillis. "It was not natural," states Jordan. "And she was the first: Phillis Miracle: Phillis Miracle Wheatley: the first Black human being to be published in America. She was the second female to be published in America" (89).

In *Notes,* Jefferson dismisses Wheatley's first volume of poetry, *Poems on Various Subjects Religious and Moral,* published in London in 1773, as "below the dignity of criticism" (140). Although Jordan does not address Jefferson's comment directly, her essay on Wheatley redresses both his assessment and the standards according to which it was made and perpetuated. Jordan concedes that some of Wheatley's poetry, written as it was in an alien place, in the imposed language and poetic conventions of those who "owned" her, and in tribute to the masters, is "especially awful, virtually absurd" (92). Yet "now and again and again these surviving works of the genius Phillis Wheatley veer incisive and unmistakeable, completely away from the verse of good girl Phillis" (93). And when they make this swerve, it is in celebration of liberty and the promise of the American Revolution; it is in tribute to those who would die in the struggle for freedom.

The following, a poignant and powerful poem to America's struggle against tyranny, is intensified when read in light of Wheatley's enslavement:

No more America in mournful strain
Of wrongs, and grievance unredress'd complain,
No longer shalt Thou dread the iron chain,
Which wanton tyranny with lawless head
Had made, and with it meant t'enslave the land.
Should you, my Lord, while you peruse my song,
Wonder from whence my love of Freedom sprung,
Whence flow these wishes for the common good,
By feeling hearts alone best understood,
I, young in life, by seeming cruel of fate
Was snatch'd from Afric's fancy'd happy seat.
What pangs excruciating must molest
What sorrows labour in my parent's breast?

Steel'd was that soul and by no misery mov'd
That from a father seized his babe belov'd
Such, such my case. And can I then but pray
Others may never feel tyrannic sway?
> "To the Right Honorable William, Earl of
> Dartmouth, His Majesty's Principal Secretary of
> State for North America, etc."

Wheatley's irony in wishing on America the freedom it denies her doubles back to condemn tyrannical slaveowners. The opening phrase, "No more America in mournful strain / Of wrongs," resounds with this doubled condemnation of British and American tyranny. The descriptions of colonial domination gain rhetorical power from the imagery of slavery, under which "dread" of the "lawless" "iron chain" is more than metaphorical. To communicate the origins of her "love of Freedom," Wheatley sets up a series of binary oppositions that underscore the fundamental opposition between freedom and enslavement. The "Feeling hearts" of those who understand oppose the "Steel'd" souls of the slave traders. Her parents' natural happiness is placed in opposition to their forced misery. And Africa as a "happy seat" contrasts with America as a seat of slavery. The final lines both reiterate and overturn these oppositions: the "I"/ "Other" opposition is a reversal of the one the slaveowners would hold, for they have made the slaves into objectified Others. Thus, the poetic "I" is the slave's assertion of her own subjectivity, a reversal of power that makes the slaveowners the Others. Finally, even that opposition is broken down in the expressed willingness of the "I" to pray for the "Others." Yet this willingness is made provisional by its interrogative form. Jefferson's finding such lines "beneath the dignity of criticism" leaves little doubt whose dignity was at stake.

Jordan's essay on Wheatley—the eleventh chapter of *On Call*—extends the genealogical record of American poetry. Without denying her first chapter's praise of Whitman as the father of New-World poetry, she accords Wheatley the status of the mother of New-World poetry and the "first decidedly American poet on this continent, Black or white, male or female" (93). Thus, she reinscribes herself into the tradition of American poetry as a descendent of Phillis Wheatley while she reinscribes the tradition itself. Black poetry in America is an etho-poetic practice of freedom that opposes the forces of domination. As Jordan writes in her own poem of tribute at the end of the chapter, Wheatley's poetry is like "The tall black trees of winter / lifting up a poetry of snow / so that we may be astounded / by the poems of Black / trees inside a cold environment" (98).

In *On Call*, Jordan records an "I" composing herself through the principle of heterogeneity, which enables her to pursue liberty by forging affinities with others. Early in the book, on the subject of South Africa, she writes, "I am only waiting for the call" (18). By the end she is, as the title suggests, on call: "I believe that we, on the American left, can become at least as bold as the pro-lifers who say they would arm freedom fighters and protect democracy, around the world. As the allies of all movements for self-determination, we need to renew our own claims to the flag—to our rightful powers of representation, and we need to assert our own pro-life policies as pro-life, identify our own freedom fighters, and stipulate our own conditions for the furtherance of democracy" (147–48). Working for self-determination is a self-constitutive activity for specific intellectuals ethically engaged in an aesthetics of liberty. To think that transformation is to follow the example of Phillis Wheatley, in whose nightly dreams ideas ranged "Licentious and unbounded o'er the plains."[4]

As Jordan locates herself within the heterogeneous lineage of Wheatley and Whitman, she also writes of her specific and multiple positions within the major technologies of power in modern America. Through normalization these technologies of the family, sexuality, and education produce the illusion of a coherent and homogeneous identity. But such coherency is susceptible to breakdown. Rather than reinforcing illusory coherence or giving way to paralyzing fragmentation, *On Call* promotes practices through which the totalizing impositions of coherence and homogeneity may be questioned and aesthetic-ethical identities shaped.

Several chapters in *On Call* show how dominant power relations are localized in the territory of the female body. These essays remap bodily terrains, opening the borders demarcated through normalization. One of the most moving is "Many Rivers to Cross," which describes the night that Jordan's mother committed suicide. Events leading up to that night had brought Jordan back to her parents' home, divorced, without money, with a son to support, and suffering from the effects of a poorly executed illegal abortion (she explains that to terminate the pregnancy actually required three abortions).

Her subjectivity is thus intersected by several forces of the deployments of alliance and sexuality: those of the family power structure, in which she is both daughter and divorced mother; of the socioeconomic power structure, in which she is a black woman worker and a mother of a child whose paternal support is not enforced by law; and of the heterosexist power structure, which denies women reproductive freedom. The difficulties of these circumstances are compounded by her mother's physical impairment by a severe stroke, which has left her weakened and unable to care for herself or her husband, Jordan's father.

What Jordan describes is, in other words, a situation of disorder brought on by several breaks in the lines of force that maintain the power network of a normalized and normalizing society. This disorder reaches a dramatic peak the night her mother takes her own life, a disorder represented in her father's inability to discern whether her mother is dead or alive. Jordan describes her father coming to her room in the middle of the night: " 'It's your mother,' he told me, in a burly, formal voice. 'I think she's dead, but I'm not sure' " (22). Jordan descends the stairs:

> "Momma?!" I called, aloud. At the edge of the cot, my mother was leaning forward, one arm braced to hoist her body up. She was trying to stand up! I rushed over. "Wait. Here, I'll help you!" I said. (23)

But she arrives too late to help her mother. The police arrive and reveal that her mother's death was suicide. Her father informs her that her mother has left insurance money in her name, but he refuses to give it to her. In a fight that breaks out between Jordan and her father, her body begins to hemorrhage, a result of the abortions, and Jordan is hospitalized (22–24).

This essay shows how an art of remembrance, especially remembrance of the death of a parent, may be understood within the ethical tradition of an aesthetics of liberty. Jordan reflects on what that night means to her:

> And I think all of this is really about women and work. Certainly this is all about me as a woman and my life work. I mean I am not sure my mother's suicide was something extraordinary. Perhaps most women must deal with a similar inheritance, the legacy of a woman whose death you cannot possibly pinpoint because she died so many, many times and because, even before she became your mother, the life of that woman was taken; I say it was taken away. (26)

Jordan ends her essay with regret that she "came too late to help [her] mother to her feet" but with an affirmation about the "new women's work," a work in which "we will not die trying to stand up: we will live that way: standing up" (26).

For American women, and especially for those who have been marginalized by poverty, race, or ethnicity, to live "standing up" is to refuse the identity demanded by the power network of American society. An example of the new women's work is the everyday assistance Jordan describes coming from other women who helped her "to stay alive." Like Jefferson, Jordan advocates an ethics of health care in opposition to practices of hospitalization that breed dependency and disease. The women who came to Jordan's aid—Mrs. Hazel Griffin and Jordan's cousin Valerie—helped her in the care of the self, assisting her in the process of self-determination by preparing food, watching her son, and helping her set up a place to live. Their ethics was concerned with the health of the self and with instilling in others, as much as possible, a capacity for self-care. Thus, Jordan makes women's traditional duties of nurturance a vital practice for all individuals. Also part of the new women's work is writing, which gives new meanings to their lives. Such is Jordan's work as a specific intellectual, in this instance challenging the value system of the patriarchal, normalized family insofar as it fosters docility and medicalization rather than the care of the self. Both of these forms of life-work are key practices in an aesthetics of liberty.

On Call shows how the illusion of coherent, normalized subjectivity breaks down at moments of crisis: although forces of normalization move centripetally toward the construction of a unified subjectivity, in practice one is never established as belonging essentially and exclusively to one meaning system. Rather, one is individualized as female or male, black or white or Asian, American or Italian or Nicaraguan, a daughter or both a mother and a daughter, married or divorced or single, living alone or with others, wealthy or poor or managing, Jewish or Catholic or Buddhist, lesbian or heterosexual or bisexual or celibate, young or old or middle-aged, and so on. In short, the "I" itself is heterogeneous. These diverse constitutive modes of subjectivity are sites not only of normalization but of resistance. "Report from the Bahamas" discusses the ways in which the heterogeneous relations of selfhood may provide unexpected affinities with others that facilitate the practice of liberty. Such affinity formations are necessary in order to continue to reformulate knowledge and subjectivity, that is, to prevent the settling-in of domination.

"Report from the Bahamas" begins by cataloguing the many disjunctures of class, race, and gender Jordan experiences on a vacation in the Bahamas, during which she stayed at the Sheraton British Colonial. She quotes the Ministry of Tourism's history, which she finds in her hotel room: "New World History begins on the same day that modern Bahamian history begins— October 12, 1492. . . . After the Revolutions, American Loyalists fled from the newly independent states and settled in the

Bahamas. Confederate blockade-runners used the island as a haven during the War between the States, and after the War, a number of Southerners moved to the Bahamas" (39–40). This account ignores the history of blacks on the Bahamas, thus repeating the devaluation of a people that had been subjugated through colonialist expansion. And yet, as Jordan indicates, as a tourist she is part of that colonialism, enjoying a room cleaned by a black Bahamian woman, eating poolside meals brought by a black Bahamian man, purchasing gifts crafted by the Bahamian working poor. This, she states, "is my consciousness of race and class and gender identity. . . . They sell and I buy or I don't. They risk not eating. I risk going broke on my first vacation afternoon" (41).

Where is the unity of gender to be found between the basket-weavers and the women who buy their baskets? Where is the race solidarity between the black food-workers and the black tourists who eat the food they have prepared? "So far as I can see," Jordan argues, "the usual race and class concepts of connection, or gender assumptions of unity, do not apply very well. I doubt if they ever did. Otherwise why would black folks forever bemoan our lack of solidarity when the deal turns real. And if unity on the basis of sexual oppression is something natural, then why do we women, the majority people on the planet, still have a problem?" (46). Furthermore, to assume solidarity on the basis of presumed natural connections obscures not only real differences but real similarities among people. For example, Agee's humanistic perception of the poor as simply a less fortunate version of the privileged ensnares him in an attempt to speak for them instead of listening to them and helping them to speak for themselves. His unconscious class bias imposes an artificial similarity between classes and obsures their more fundamental similarity in the will to self-determination. Likewise, as Jordan points out, the "usual Women's Studies curriculum" makes this mistake in its "white procession of independently well-to-do writers (Gertrude Stein/ Virginia Woolf/Hilda Doolittle are standard names among the 'essential' women writers)" (44). As a result, differing and conflicting views are not heard. And this kind of exclusion leads to a second: the missing of opportunities for connections that derive from sources not exclusively defined by gender, race, or class.

In the second half of this chapter, Jordan addresses the possibilities for forging such affinity groups. The example she cites shows the complexity of women's lives in the intersections of the deployments of alliance and sexuality, a complexity that involves but transcends the categories of race, class, and gender. Jordan relates a story about one of the students in a women's poetry class she taught. After class the student, a young black South African with an abusive, alcoholic husband, sought her help. Jordan explains that she knew both the wife and the husband through a campus group supporting the liberation struggles in southern Africa. "What about this presumable connection: this husband and this wife fled from that homeland of hatred against them, and now what? He was destroying himself. If not stopped, he would certainly murder his wife" (48).

Lacking institutional resources—revealing gaps in the normalizing network of bio-power—Jordan reports finding help from an unexpected source, an Irish woman in the poetry class. The Irish woman's experiences with an alcoholic father who battered her mother became a point of connection between these two young women who might otherwise have been caught up in the Irish-black antagonisms of America. Their point of connection was a site of resistance against both the physical abuse of women sanctioned by the deployment of alliance and the medicalizing expertise by which women are subjected in deployment of sexuality. It was, as well, a forging of an ethics that extends the field of freedom.

As a university professor, Jordan is herself part of the expertise of the American educational system, another of the primary mechanisms of normalizing bio-power and hence a primary site of resistance to that power. As her discussion about the South African student who was also an abused wife indicates, Jordan's role as a feminist professor creates a disjuncture in the disciplinary powers of the educational system. And as a black professor of English, she occupies another site of potential disjuncture, this one arising from the system's normalizing exclusion of black English in favor of "standard English." Three chapters of *On Call* critique the imperialistic model of language, the regime of truth it produces, and the subjectivity it constructs. As Jordan shows, the institutionalization of a standard language reinforces pedagogical normalization and surveillance with mechanisms of self-surveillance, as students learn to write and speak themselves into standardized subjectivity. In these three chapters, she develops and enacts a counterposition on the teaching of language, a position consonant with an aesthetic ethics of self-stylization.[5]

"Problems of Language in a Democratic State" challenges the view that language problems in America are black problems with language. Such a view holds that all is well with the educational system and that black children (or Hispanic or Asian-American, etc.) are at fault. This racist view has become less tenable in the face of a general decline in reading and writing skills throughout the country. As Jordan states, "every university in the nation now recognizes that most of its students seriously lack those analytical abilities that devolve from disciplined and critical and confident and regular exercise of the mind" (29). However, a distinction should be made between Jordan's concept of discipline and the concept promoted by the pedagogy of normalizing power relations (sometimes referred to as disciplinary power relations). As all of the works discussed in this book illustrate, the tradition of an aesthetics of liberty customarily has advocated educational rigor—but to foster individual critical capacities, not to impose a standardized body of knowledge.

In explaining how the general decline in American education has occurred, Jordan first explains how it occurred for black children. "Mostly Black kids ran into a censorship of their living particular truth, past and present":

What those children brought into the classroom: their language, their style, their sense of humor, their ideas of smart, their music,

their need for a valid history and a valid literature—history and
literature that included their faces and their voices—and serious
teachers who would tell them, "C'mon, I see you. Let me give
you a hand,"—all of this was pretty well ridiculed and rejected,
or denied to them. (29)

What was initially seen—and ignored—as a black problem soon
became a national problem; and Jordan points out that the national problem has the same root: the imposed homogeneity of
the English language.

The homogeneity of abstract, standardized, passive-voiced English as an official language normalizes students, making them
into docile, unquestioning citizens. "When will a legitimate-
ly American language," Jordan demands in sweeping, Whit-
manesque fashion, "a language including Nebraska, Harlem,
New Mexico, Oregon, Puerto Rico, Alabama and working-class
life and freeways and Pac-Man become the language studied and
written and glorified in the classroom? . . . Who teaches white
kids to think for themselves? Who has ever wanted white children to see their own faces, clearly, to hear their own voices,
clearly?" (30). Learning to speak through one's own diversities
and having access to the diversities of others is necessary for the
practice of democracy. Jordan proposes multiculturalist principles for a non-normalizing pedagogy: "If we lived in a democratic state our language would have to hurtle, fly, curse, and
sing, in all the common American names, all the undeniable and
representative and participating voices of everybody here. . . .
We would make our language conform to the truth of our many
selves and we would make our language lead us into the equality
of power that a democratic state must represent" (30). Insisting
on official English at the expense of other languages—on an exclusive and exclusionary white, class-privileged, masculinist English—is an act of collaboration with domination.

Jordan takes her refusal of that collaboration into the classroom in the chapter entitled "Nobody Mean More to Me Than
You And the Future Life of Willie Jordan." When black students
in her course (entitled "In Search of the Invisible Black Woman")

expressed discomfort in reading the dialect of *The Color Purple,* Jordan prompted them to reflect on why they should be so alienated from the print manifestation of a language they themselves spoke. Realizing that the suppression of black English was an extinction of their culture and their way of seeing the world, they asked Jordan to teach them to write their own language. This led her to teach a course the following year called "The Art of Black English"—probably, as Jordan remarks, the first such course ever offered in the United States.

This chapter provides a handbook of Rules and Guidelines for black English. In parody of normative handbooks for standard English that codify a vast number of grammatical practices, Jordan's minimalist handbook (four Rules and eighteen Guidelines) encourages personal innovation, including the invention of such words as "astropotamous," which "means huge like a hippo plus astronomical and, therefore, signifies real big" (132). The four Rules encapsulate black English's resistance to disciplinary codification and reiterate the importance of self-stylization in language:

> Rule 1: *Black English is about a whole lot more than motha-fuckin.*

> Rule 2: *If it's wrong in Standard English it's probably right in Black English, or, at least, you're hot.*

> Rule 3: *If it don't sound like something that come out somebody mouth then it don't sound right. If it don't sound right then it ain't hardly right. Period.*

> Rule 4: *Forget about the spelling. Let the syntax carry you.* (128; italics hers)

Jordan points out that the oral tradition and syntax of black English constitute a consciousness (or subjectivity) that valorizes the speaker's activity (virtually no passive construction), the strong sense of personal voice, and the ideal of communicating (as opposed to obfuscating) one's ideas. Such values, in keeping with an ethics of self-stylization, oppose the ideal of the coherent, homogeneous, abstract subjectivity constructed through standard English.

During the semester, the class's resistance to the disciplinary forces of compulsory standard English ran up against a complex network of overlapping power relations between the police, legal services, and the public media. This occurred after the police killed Reggie Jordan, the brother of Willie Jordan, one of the students in the class. Jordan describes her efforts to garner community support to help Willie Jordan's family pay for a possible suit against the police, a venture so costly that only the wealthy can undertake it. But except for an article in *The Village Voice*, the media refused to cover the shooting of Reggie Jordan. With permission from Willie Jordan, she then presented the case to her class. "We had talked about the politics of language. We had talked about love and sex and child abuse and men and women," Jordan writes, but "the murder of Reggie Jordan broke like a hurricane across the room" (134).

Jordan reports that, in the discussion that ensued, the students decided to write letters of condolence to the Jordan family and letters of outrage to the police. They readily decided to write to the Jordans in black English. But the question about which language to use to confront the police proved agonizing:

> How best to serve the memory of Reggie Jordan? Should we use the language of the killers—Standard English—in order to make our ideas acceptable to those controlling the killers? But wouldn't what we had to say be rejected, summarily, if we said it in our own language, the language of the victim, Reggie Jordan? But if we sought to express ourselves by abandoning our language wouldn't that mean our suicide on top of Reggie's murder? But if we expressed ourselves in our own language wouldn't that be suicidal to the wish to communicate with those who, evidently, did not give a damn about us/Reggie/police violence in the Black community? (135)

The students finally decided to write their letters to the police, together with a collectively composed opening paragraph, "inthe language of Reggie Jordan" (136) and to send them to *Newsday*.

"*Newsday* rejected the piece," Jordan reports. "*The Village Voice* could not find room in their 'Letters' section to print the individual messages from the students to the police. None of the tv news reporters picked up the story. Nobody raised $180,000 to prosecute the murder of Reggie Jordan. Reggie Jordan is really dead" (137).

The chapter does not conclude with this forced silence but, rather, with an essay written by Willie Jordan in which he explains the links he has come to see between systematic police brutality in the United States and in South Africa. "Many Africans die each year as a result of the deliberate use of police force to protect the white power structure," he writes, and continues, "I recently received a painful reminder that racism, poverty, and the abuse of power are global problems which are by no means unique to South Africa" (137–38). Combining the conventions of standard English with the political ethos of black English, Willie Jordan records his brother's death in words that defy the police records and turn their documentation into a ground for resistance to injustice:

> I honestly believe that the Police Department's assessment of my brother's murder is nothing short of ABSOLUTE BULLSHIT, and thus far no evidence has been produced to alter perception of the situation. . . . Part of the argument of the officers who shot Reggie was that he had attacked one of them and took his gun. . . . According to the Death Certificate and autopsy report, Reggie was shot eight times from point-blank range. The Doctor who performed the autopsy told me himself that two bullets entered the side of my brother's head, four bullets were sprayed into his back, and two bullets struck him in the back of his legs. It is obvious that unnecessary force was used by the police and that it is extremely difficult to shoot someone in his back when he is attacking or approaching you. (138)

Willie Jordan ends his essay with an assertion of the value of continued resistance in the face of the dominant forms of power: "Although it is a difficult task, we do have the power to make a change" (139).

As part of that effort toward change, the next chapter in *On Call* uses black English throughout. It is a political analysis of "White Tuesday": election day, 1984. Both this analysis and the story of Reggie Jordan point to the intersection of the law with other technologies of normalizing bio-power, particularly those operating through the military, the police, the schools, and the electoral process. Jordan opens her discussion with the observation: "Whole campaign an' dint neither one of them joker talk about right or wrong. We knowed it was trouble" (141). Part of the trouble is the "astropotamous story about apartheid an' South Africa" that candidate number one tells (142). ("Number One love him some camera" [141].) Number one "say progress somehow. He say listen close now how the U.S.A. ain' no asylum for no freedom fighters lessen they on the payroll. He not studyin' no justice. He say nothin' about blood" (142). In short, the rhetoric of progress, superbly suited to bio-power's administration of life, conceals the unjust operations of the law.

Jordan's analyses serve as crucial reminders that the proliferating technologies of bio-power have not thoroughly replaced the technologies of the deployment of alliance and that *both* forms—alliance and bio-power—are currently installed in American imperialism. Although bio-power is itself bloodless (Foucault, *History of Sexuality* 144), *On Call* demonstrates how its calculated administration of lives and its enticing rhetoric of socioeconomic development conceal the blood that is shed domestically and globally in the name of American progress and justice. Police regulatory power left Reggie Jordan dead. The army's bloodless bio-power slogan, "Be all you can be," must be understood in the context of the bloody suppression of self-determination in such places as Nicaragua. As the chapters entitled "South Africa: Bringing it All Back Home" and "Black Folks on Nicaragua: 'Leave Those Folks Alone!' " indicate, black Americans know all too well the meaning of the song Jordan hears a five-year-old Nicaraguan girl singing:

> see what the man have done (done)
> see how the red blood run (run) (55)

Jordan's discussions of American foreign policy in Central America, the Middle East, and South Africa show the ways in which bio-power and the law intersect in "humanitarian" aid to the Contras, in economic aid to countries in alliance with South Africa, and in South African investment portfolios held by American institutions of higher education.

Jordan concludes with a call to Americans to resist the "United States' collaboration with the enemies of self-determination" (145) and to assist the struggles for liberty. *"As we oppose aid to the contras, let us also propose massive foreign aid to the Sandinista government. As we oppose investment in South Africa, let us also propose massive foreign aid to the frontline states of Angola and Mozambique"* (147; italics hers). The American Revolution would not have been won without this kind of aid from America's allies of freedom. In commemoration of its own struggle against colonial domination, Jordan calls on Americans to come to the support of global democracy.

Jordan's work in *On Call* is the self-scrutinizing, non-normalizing production of truth. Such work exemplifies Foucault's view that the "task of telling the truth is an endless labor: to respect it in all its complexity is an obligation which no power can do without—except by imposing the silence of slavery" ("The Concern for Truth" 267). Laboring to tell the truth in its complexity and heterogeneity is a struggle against the dominant and domineering forms of power that either impose silence or demand that we echo hegemonic truth.[6] Specific intellectuals like Kingston and Jordan, writing from the places of their marginalization, express truth with a complexity that normalizing power rules out. As this study of texts that promote an ethics of an aesthetics of liberty attempts to show, such intellectual labor is vital to American democracy. The history of America indicates that ethical-political problems of freedom require more than a revolution to solve them. They require an ethos of everyday life—whereby individuals engage in practices of liberty.[7]

As inherited forms of religious and legal morality continue to lose influence, as late-capitalist forces produce fragmentation and confusion in individual identity, and as the human sciences, aided by global media technologies, gain ascendancy, the search for principles upon which to base an ethics is increasingly vulnerable to the forces of normalizing bio-power with their beguiling promises to regulate an unruly world. But America's ethical aesthetics of liberty has its own strong tradition of opposition to domination, its own proliferating power, and its own appealing promise of greater freedom. The ethics Jefferson inaugurated in the Declaration of Independence and elaborated in *Notes* proclaimed the freedom of the subject and the care of the self as arts of living. Because such an ethics is grounded in aesthetics, it does not propose a discoverable, unchanging truth. On the contrary, it promotes practices of liberty and self-stylization that enable people to transform themselves and truth. Such an ethos espouses an always ongoing, often discordant activity of thought in which assumptions—one's own and those of others—are continually confronted, examined, and recast. To do otherwise—to accept the regime of truth that has been constituted by the normalizing forces of bio-power—is to collaborate with forces that negate democratic freedom.

NOTES

NOTES TO THE INTRODUCTION

1. Michel Foucault uses the term "founders of discursivity" to describe the ways in which authors like Marx and Freud initiated a discourse that includes not only their own writings but the "subsequent transformations" that emerge from (but are not prescribed by) them. "[T]hey both have established an endless possibility of discourse" ("What is an Author?" 114–15).

2. The term *technology* used in this sense is from the Greek *technē*, which indicates a practical rationality guided by a goal (rather than the narrower meaning of technology as applied sciences). Foucault outlines four major types of technologies, "each a matrix of practical reason," which might be analyzed: "(1) technologies of production, which permit us to produce, transform, or manipulate things; (2) technologies of sign systems, which permit us to use signs, meanings, symbols, or signification; (3) technologies of power, which determine the conduct of individuals and submit them to certain ends or domination, an objectivizing of the subject; (4) technologies of the self, which permit individuals to effect by their own means or with the help of others a certain number of operations on their own bodies and souls, thoughts, conduct, and way of being, so as to transform themselves in order to attain a certain state of happiness, purity, wisdom, perfection, or immortality" ("Technologies" 18).

3. For Foucault's discussions of technologies of normalization, see *Discipline and Punish* and *The History of Sexuality;* for his speculations about the care of the self as a contemporary ethical practice, see the interview entitled "The Ethic of Care for the Self as a Practice of Freedom" in *The Final Foucault.*

4. Because of its resistance to dominant forms of truth, power, and ethics, America's aesthetics of liberty is similar to what John Rajchman has identified as Foucault's ethics. In Foucault's modern "art of living," Rajchman observes, beauty is an ethical category, but, rather than holding to an ideal of harmony between oneself and the " 'spaces' in which

we can become what is natural," this ethics sees "dissonance or disharmony between one's given nature and one's possibilities of existence, between one's identity and what one can see in oneself and in the process going on around one. . . . In this art the events one sees going on around one interrupt one's sense of one's self and cause one to think and rethink" (Rajchman 114).

5. Emerson is perhaps the most obvious "missing" figure in this study. For a number of reasons I have chosen not to write a chapter on Emerson. Although his texts do present many of the elements comprised by an aesthetics of liberty, I think that, to a greater extent than with texts by Jefferson, Fuller, and Thoreau, Emerson's texts tend to veer away from personal and societal issues and toward cosmic ones. Correspondingly, his use of beauty as an ethical category becomes universal and totalizing rather than critical. Hence, Fuller and Thoreau provided greater challenges to the normalizing power relations taking hold in their time period.

6. In *The Unusable Past: Theory and the Study of American Literature*, Russell J. Reising discusses the exclusivity of the American literary canon and makes a compelling case for studying works that have been designated "unusable." The same points could be made about the canons of philosophy and political theory. Moreover, the notion of a disciplinary canon is itself a power/knowledge formation that perpetuates the exclusion of texts that challenge the status quo. I would also add that we must be wary of interpretations of canonized works like *Walden*, which have been made usable by being depoliticized.

NOTES TO CHAPTER ONE

1. Richard Rorty has argued that Jefferson "set the tone for American liberal politics" by helping to "make respectable the idea that politics can be separated from beliefs about matters of ultimate importance—that shared beliefs among citizens on such matters [as religion] are not essential to a democratic society" ("The Priority of Democracy to Philosophy" 279). While I agree with the last part of Rorty's claim—that a Jeffersonian democracy must not require that all citizens share beliefs—I do not read Jefferson as separating politics from beliefs in the way Rorty suggests. This study departs from Rorty's adherence to a private/public demarcation between beliefs and politics.

Part of the problem in Rorty's discussion is the conflation of beliefs in general and of religious beliefs in particular. Jefferson explicitly espoused the separation of church and state, but such a view does not entail separation of politics from (possibly undisclosed) ethical beliefs. Also see note 4 below.

2. In discussing Jefferson's aim of happiness I draw from my 1982 essay "Thomas Jefferson: The Virtue of Aesthetics and the Aesthetics of Virtue" and from the revisionist work of Garry Wills and Richard Matthews. The argument in this chapter and in the earlier essay accord more with Matthews's understanding of the aesthetic element of Jefferson's moral philosophy than with Wills's notion of a sentimentalist Jefferson employing a "science of morality" (164).

3. Richard Matthews gives an excellent account of the importance of the doctrines of Epicurus, Jesus, and Epictetus for Jefferson's political theory in the chapter in his *Radical Politics of Thomas Jefferson* called "Jeffersonian Government: Public and Private Happiness."

4. For a discussion of Jefferson's refusal to make public or even divulge to his family his religious beliefs, see Eugene R. Sheridan's introduction to *Jefferson's Extracts from the Gospels*.

5. Historians have shown the influences on Jefferson of the writings of Lord Kames and Francis Hutcheson (Peterson 55, Chinard 258, Sheehan 28–29, Wills 298). The third earl of Shaftesbury's *Characteristics of Men, Manners, Morals, Opinions, Times* (1711) provided Jefferson with arguments for the separation of church and state that he used in his Bill for Religious Freedom as well as an aesthetic approach to morality derived from the ancient Greeks (Quinby 340–47).

6. My narrative of the history of *Notes* is drawn from William Peden's introduction to his invaluable edition of Jefferson's *Notes*.

7. Garry Wills's discussion about the passage on the Natural Bridge, though illuminating in its explication of sublimity, struggles against itself to maintain the thesis that for Jefferson sublimity was essentially a matter of scientific observation. Although he points out that Jefferson's observations of the Natural Bridge proceed from Science to Nature to Art (in contrast to the observations of Chastellux, which proceed, as Wills notes, from Nature to Art to Science) Wills argues that the experience of sublimity was a scientific observation for Jefferson. He bases his argument on the assertion that "when men of Jefferson's generation talked of sublimity . . . , they were bound to think of one man's theory"—Burke's 1757 *Philosophical Enquiry into the Origins of Our Ideas of*

the Sublime and Beautiful. Burke was "rigorous in his logic and reductionism," and therefore, Wills argues, so was Jefferson (Wills 259–72). It is, however, neither surprising that Jefferson used the word *sublime* nor necessary that he had Burke in mind when he did (indeed, he may have). What is worth noting is that the passage in *Notes* moves from Science to Nature to Art.

8. Although this depiction helps Jefferson argue that corrupt law is avoidable, it is, like any idealization, reductive: Native Americans become an Other, somehow simultaneously benign and savage.

9. For an extended discussion of the contradictions and ambivalences in Jefferson's treatment of blacks, see in particular the chapter entitled "Thomas Jefferson: Self and Society" in Winthrop Jordan's crucial work, *White Over Black: American Attitudes Toward the Negro, 1550–1812*.

10. Such an argument would have been unlikely, of course. In fact, the word *miscegenation* itself was not coined until 1864, which gives us some indication of how unsettling the idea was to white Americans.

NOTES TO CHAPTER TWO

1. Also see Lauren Berlant's excellent discussion of the ways in which this kind of discourse, which she calls the "female complaint," serves "to mediate and manage the social contradictions that arise from women's sexual and affective allegiance to a phallocentric ideology that has, in practice, denied women power, privilege, and presence in the public and private spheres" (243).

2. Also see Marie Mitchell Olesen Urbanski's pioneering exploration of *Woman in the Nineteenth Century*. Urbanski argues that the structure of *Woman* is that of the sermon and oration combined; that, rhetorically, Fuller makes connections between her own experiences and those of women in general; that her tone is conversational, expressing the "spoken word"; that her imagery is organic; and that examples from literature, history, religion, and mythology lend authority to her argument.

3. As David Robinson has argued, Fuller's "complex dialectic" is one in which "the ideal demands embodiment while the process of social transformation must have the guidance of an ideal. Fuller, who em-

bodied her ideal in the commitment to self-culture, discovered that self-culture as an end required social reform as a means, that the fulfillment of woman necessitated the concerted action of women" (96).

4. A helpful discussion of the limits of a feminist androgyny model appears in Alison M. Jaggar's *Feminist Politics and Human Nature,* on pages 85–88 in particular.

5. It is interesting to compare Fuller's concept of the Virgin-Mother with Florence Nightingale's call for a female Christ. Nightingale was not a supporter of suffrage or even of equal educational rights. However, in "Cassandra" (written in 1852), she challenged the Victorian ideal of the perfect lady and depicted marriage itself as destructive to women, saying it drove them to idleness and sometimes to madness. Cassandra, of course, was the prophet of truth who was fated to be misunderstood.

6. In *The Subjection of Women,* John Stuart Mill described a redeemed future in which marriage would be a unity of equals. Also like Fuller, he drew on a virgin figure: Virgil's Astraea, whose return, as Susan Hardy Aiken indicates, was to signify "the establishment of an earthly paradise" (Aiken 365).

7. In an insightful discussion of Elizabeth Barrett Browning's personal, political, and artistic struggles, Sandra Gilbert places Margaret Fuller in a tradition of women writers who "imagined nothing less than the transformation of *patria* into *matria* and the risorgimento of the lost community of women that Rosetti called the 'mother country.' " For Barrett Browning, this mother country was a liberated Italy in which both men and women would be free. Gilbert adds that this was Fuller's view as well.

NOTES TO CHAPTER THREE

1. John D'Emilio and Estelle Freedman provide a useful survey of this social change in *Intimate Matters.* David Leverenz's *Manhood and the American Renaissance* is the most extended study of the ideology of American masculinity during this period. Although I do not hold to his psychoanalytic approach to the authors he analyzes, his readings of their works offer important insights into the discourses of masculinity. Also see Leonard Neufeldt's examination of *Walden* as a parody of young men's guidebooks. The list of critical works on Thoreau and

chastity would be too long to give here, but critics who have helped me formulate my analysis include Charles Anderson, James Armstrong, Mary Elkins Moller, and Ross Pudaloff. Of these, only Pudaloff employs a Foucauldian method of analysis (in disagreement with a psychological approach).

2. Also see Walter Benn Michaels's compelling discussion of *Walden*'s oscillation between "the value of the hard bottom" and the value of "bottomlessness," a contradiction he says critics often try to resolve through appeals to unity.

3. Ever since *Walden*'s publication in 1854, this evocative disclosure has tantalized readers and prompted numerous attempts at explication. The fundamental opposition between three important scholarly treatments of the hound, horse, and dove suggest how varied the findings of critics have been. In 1937, Edith Peairs suggested that the three figures, which she argued Thoreau had borrowed from Voltaire, revealed that Thoreau was "disillusioned in his search of the ideal friend" (868). Challenging Peairs some two decades later, Frank Davidson argued that the "freshness, beginnings, growth, renewal, change" throughout *Walden* are testimony that there "is not much disillusionment" in the work (522–24). Davidson's analysis of the hound, horse, and dove as "symbols of a wildness that keeps man in touch with nature, intellectual stimulus, and purification of spirit," respectively, is closer to my analysis of the figures' thematic roles in *Walden*. But in dismissing thematic disillusionment, he relinquished the notion of ambiguity so crucial to Thoreau's ethics. More recently, Barbara Johnson has argued that, "in order to communicate the irreducibly particular yet ultimately unreadable nature of loss, Thoreau has chosen to use three symbols that clearly *are* symbols but that do not really symbolize anything outside themselves" (53). Although I take her point that "we can never be absolutely sure" about the "rhetorical status of any given image" (55–56), Thoreau provides many clues for developing myriad meanings associated with the three figures. More than the unreadability of loss, I think *Walden* emphasizes the multiple readability of regaining and/or creating chastity. This multiple readability defies the strict classification systems of the deployment of sexuality.

4. The next reference to a dog may be read as a lighthearted pun. In "The Ponds," Thoreau describes White Pond, Walden's "lesser twin," in the following way: "As at Walden, in sultry *dog-day* weather, looking

down through the woods on some of its *bays* which are not so deep but that the reflection from the bottom tinges them, its waters are of a misty bluish-green or glaucous color" (197). I relegate this reference to the notes out of a fear of appearing to see dog imagery everywhere (the emphasis is mine). The discussion of White Pond's primitivism does, however, seem to support my general point that allusions to the hound signify primitive existence.

5. Critics have been divided on Thoreau's attitude toward the "wild." Some have seen his veneration of the spiritual at the end of "Higher Laws" as a betrayal of his claim to love the "wild not less than the good." Frederick Garber's judgment is perhaps the most extreme: he calls the whole of the chapter "markedly schizophrenic." Disagreeing with Sherman Paul, Joseph Wood Krutch, and Charles Anderson, who diminish Thoreau's ambivalence by seeing the chapter's movement as developmental, Garber argues that the "disgust, the hiatus, and the argument for equality and continuity of reverence all make it impossible to support a developmental reading of the chapter. . . . Rather, these factors point to an ambivalence so profound and unsettling that Thoreau could get around it only by a disjunctive maneuver which avoids confrontation of the contradictory positions" (120–21). I would argue that Thoreau deals much more explicitly with the wild/good problematic than Garber allows and that he does so in a way that confirms the thesis that "Higher Laws" and *Walden* are developmental in vision, albeit precariously so. In short, what Garber labels ambivalence, I would describe as Thoreau's portrayal of life's multiplicity, that is, his recognition that nature and human existence are variously interpretable and therefore resistant to mastery and control.

6. Also see Leonard Neufeldt's discussion of the good and the beautiful in regard to *Walden*'s moral aestheticism.

7. Critics tend to equivocate on the respective importance of spring and summer to *Walden*. F. O. Matthiessen's *American Renaissance,* for example, is somewhat contradictory. He states, on one hand, that "the last movement is the advance to 'Spring' " but observes just a few sentences later that Thoreau "foreshortens and condenses the twenty-six months to the interval from the beginning of one summer to the next" (170). Matthiessen's emphasis on spring as an "advance" stresses transcendence over ongoing self-stylization. This tendency is even stronger in J. Lyndon Shanley's *The Making of Walden.* In a discussion of the

structuring of *Walden* by seasons, Shanley first notes that summer closes the work, although he emphasizes spring's "triumphant tone" (80–81). He then contradicts himself by remarking on "the chronology beginning with the summer and ending with the spring" (82). In *The Shores of America,* Sherman Paul also stresses spring and rebirth as the closing themes of *Walden.* Initially Paul argues that summer was for Thoreau the least welcome season, "the season when he felt his impurity most" (282). Later, however, he revises this position somewhat, stating that summer was "the season in which [Thoreau's] senses were all alive, the season of external and outdoor life, when there were no barriers to communion, when he enjoyed the bloom of the present moment" (327). Despite this reading, Paul ends his discussion of *Walden* by emphasizing spring and rebirth.

NOTES TO CHAPTER FOUR

1. My discussion draws on the ideas of a number of critics who discuss the ways in which *Let Us* uses certain genres against themselves. Alan Holder locates the work within the documentary category but asserts that it "may be seen as at once the climactic example of, and the grand antithesis to" the documentary (191). William Stott also treats the work as a type of documentary expression, but one that has " 'corrected' documentary, transformed a strategy of social polemic, of propaganda, into something—'call it art if you must,' sneered Agee— capable of permanent revelations of the spirit" (25). Stott's discussions of both the photographic and the written texts are excellent.

Eugene Chesnick takes up the question why Agee rejected fiction as a vehicle for relating his experiences with the tenants. He concludes that Agee sought "a sense of his own identity and at the same time to reach out to identify with others. Such identification is not appropriate for the purposes of fiction" (67). Linda Ray Pratt adds that conventional journalistic forms were no more appropriate to Agee's subject than novelistic ones. Rather than assigning *Let Us* to a specific genre, she argues that the work was "shaped in the quarrel between Agee's values and those of his historical time," and that, in "the struggle for an appropriate form, the subject is reshaped, refocused, and reinterpreted by the writer's own sensibility and response to history until what was once merely subject becomes what we may call content. The very act of defining and embodying the content creates the form" (96, 84). Finally, Robert Zaller focuses on the self-revelatory features of the book, calling it a "ruthlessly unsparing autobiography and one of the most sustained meditations on the relations between conscience and knowledge in our language" (154).

2. Although I treat Evans's photography as counterespionage, I don't disagree with John Tagg's classification of it among the branches of photography that historically have served as instruments of social control through surveillance. Tagg's work is invaluable for its explorations of that problematic. Nevertheless, I think the context of Evans's presentation in *Let Us* places it in opposition to governmental surveillance.

3. As Carol Shloss notes, Agee was not unaware of the way the camera (and, by extension, film) could be used to abuse what he called truth. In his critique of Margaret Bourke-White, he pointed out that "institutions around him were involved in creating self-serving concepts of poverty and that it was their own interest in the status-quo that gave them incentive to represent the poor as repugnant and alien" (Shloss 603).

4. William Stott makes a similar point: "In a sense it is all one colon that prefaces and points the reader to reality; a colon to a text that cannot be given" (311).

5. My discussion refers to the 31 photographs appearing in the original edition of *Let Us*. The later editions contain 62 photographs and, therefore, read differently. The longer versions include a number of photographs of town scenes and townspeople, thus diverting attention away from the tenants and toward the geographic and town spaces of the rural South.

6. In a review written just after the publication of *Let Us,* Lionel Trilling praised Agee's literary accomplishment but complained of the work's "failure of moral realism," a failure that "lies in Agee's inability to see these people as anything but good," for he "writes of his people as if there were no human unregenerativeness in them, no flicker of malice or meanness, no darkness or wildness of feeling, only a sure and simple virtue, the growth, we must suppose, of their hard, unlovely poverty." Despite this reservation, Trilling assessed the work as "the most realistic and the most important moral effort of our American generation" (99–102).

7. Several critics have singled out this passage as a structuring device for the work. Kenneth Seib, who notes that the book has several

structures, argues that these "four planes might also be described as flashback, chronological narrative, imaginative reconstruction, and central consciousness. The device of flashback allowed Agee to contemplate and recall events that led up to the present moment, while chronological narrative presented events in the logical time sequence. Imaginative reconstruction differed from flashback in that the former was free to invent, to fictionally recreate in order to gain complete perspective. Finally, central consciousness was the detailed account of the perceiving mind of the artist" (48). Alfred T. Barson writes that "not only are these remarks [about the four planes] a blueprint for the book as a whole, in that sections are arranged without regard to chronological order, but they also indicate the mixture of perspectives found within any one section" (89).

8. Genevieve Moreau observes that *Let Us* is "composed like a symphony, consisting of themes and variations. Major and minor themes are introduced and repeated with modifications, now tangled, now disjointed. The variations are numerous, in either tone, movement, form, or intensity" (186–87). Picking up on Moreau's reading, Ruthann K. Johansen argues that the "rudiments of sound, rhythm, melody, and plainchant offer materials for building a cursory analysis of the book's thematic and stylistic structure. Of these, plainchant gives form to Agee's experience and reflection" (20).

9. In regard to the theme of sleep at the close of the work, Leonidas Betts states that this resolution marks "the human escape from what was from the beginning a monumental, if hopeless task" (51). Although sleep is, as Betts suggests, a form of escape, it is also a restorative.

10. J. A. Ward links the theme of silence to the work's aesthetic. The "counterpoint of sound and silence," he writes, "is the key to the form and content of the entire book." Like nature itself, music is organic because it is "self-creating," and silence is "related to religious vision." But he argues that the work's form is flawed because the last fifty pages call "attention to the unfinished and tentative nature of the book as a whole" (201–4). The open-endedness that Ward deems a flaw, I regard as part of the work's formal emulation of an ongoing aesthetics of liberty.

11. In a similar vein, James Hoopes astutely criticizes Agee for being oblivious to the tenants' sense of beauty, calling some of his treatment of them a "basic ethical problem which flawed the book" (3–4).

NOTES TO CHAPTER FIVE

1. Despite my disagreement with Eakin and Smith regarding the genre of *The Woman Warrior,* I find their readings of the work compelling and agree with their treatment of a number of textual details. Also see Patricia Lin Blinde, Suzanne Juhasz, and Jan Zlotnik Schmidt for discussions of autobiographical form and the search for self.

2. Elizabeth Bruss discusses the disappearance of autobiography in our time due to cultural changes. Such changes, which include a shift from writing to film and video, have altered "our notions of authorship, the difference between narrating (on the one hand) and perceiving or 'focalizing' (on the other), the conventions of representational realism" (299).

3. Cox makes this point in regard to Thomas Jefferson's memoirs, which he reads as part of Jefferson's efforts as an American revolutionary "to destabilize everything fixed before him" (145).

4. It is in keeping with Bakhtin's arguments to see memoirs as novelistic in their accentuation of dialogue. This is not to say that a memoir is a novel but, rather, that novelization (whether of novels or other forms) is a process by which genres move toward "liberation from all that serves as a brake on their unique development, from all that would change them along with the novel into some sort of stylization of forms that have outlived themselves" ("Epic and Novel" 39).

5. In an analysis of Simone de Beauvoir's memoirs, Kathleen Woodward comments on Estelle Jelinek's characterization of female " 'life stories' " as "more often discontinuous and fragmentary, written in a straightforward, objective manner, yet nonetheless emphasizing the personal rather than the public," saying that she (Woodward) would "reserve Jelinek's characterization of the female life story for the *memoir*" (Woodward, in Benstock, *The Private Self* 99). I generally agree but would place less stress on the memoir's emphasis of the personal over the public. Kingston's memoirs blur traditional distinctions between the personal and the public. On this point, also see Doris Sommer, "Not Just a Personal Story," in Brodzki and Schenck, *Life/Lines.*

6. For an analysis of this issue, see Biddy Martin's insightful exploration of lesbian autobiography in light of a variety of questions about generic normalization and the challenge of lesbian politics.

7. Doris Sommer underscores this point in her analysis of testimonials by Latin American women, pointing out that categorizing these

works as autobiographical tends to divert attention away from the significance of the testimonials' collective self.

8. For a feminist corrective to Foucault's neglect of the patriarchal dimensions of the deployment of sexuality, see the essays in Diamond and Quinby, *Feminism and Foucault*.

9. Kingston's *China Men* also relates the difficulties of her family in America but focuses on the men. For an analysis of the changing family power dynamics between the Chinese men and women who came to America, see Linda Ching Sledge's study of *China Men*, in which she argues that, because of the "deleterious effects of male emigration," the "mother from China is forced by the father's increasing passivity to take on 'masculine' traits of aggressiveness and authority" (10–11).

10. Kingston's use of the word "memoirs" in her subtitle also places her work alongside Simone de Beauvoir's account of resistance to bourgeois daughterhood in *Memoirs of a Dutiful Daughter*.

11. For an insightful discussion of this issue in a comparative study of *The Woman Warrior* and *The Color Purple,* see King-Kok Cheung.

12. As Foucault argues, the deployment of sexuality operates through oppositional categories of "normality" and "abnormality." The desire to attain "normality" is thus a generative function of its power network, in contrast to alliance's juridical and prohibitive mode (*History of Sexuality* 42–43).

13. Kingston reports a variation on this particular form of pedagogical domination by citing a *Teachers Newsletter* review that "gave [her] book a seventh grade reading level by using a mathematical formula of counting syllables and sentences per one hundred-word passage" ("Cultural Mis-readings" 62).

14. Woon-Ping Chin Holaday compares Ezra Pound's and Kingston's uses of the ideograph to represent their respective relationships with China. Holaday notes that in Pound's writings China tends to be "an ideal abstraction" drawn from written sources, whereas Kingston's "Chinese-American world is a tangible, changeable reality drawn from a living culture" and oral sources (19).

15. Norman Bryson argues for this distinction in painting, associating distanced time with the tradition of Western painting and displayed, processive time with the visible brushstrokes of Chinese painting (89–92).

16. Carol Gilligan's analysis of gender differences in conceptualizations of selfhood and morality associates a model of interdependence

with women at a mature stage of moral development. Her theories illuminate Kingston's depiction of an interrelational self but do not attend to cultural and ethnic differences in moral development. *The
Woman Warrior* problematizes that blind spot in Gilligan's model.

17. In *The History of Sexuality*, Foucault observes that "for us, it is
in the confession that truth and sex are joined, through the obligatory
and exhaustive expression of an individual secret" (61). And also: "The
obligation to confess is now relayed through so many different points,
is so deeply ingrained in us, that we no longer perceive it as the effect
of a power that constrains us; on the contrary, it seems to us that truth,
lodged in our most secret nature, 'demands' only to surface; that if it
fails to do so, this is because a constraint holds it in place, the violence
of a power weighs it down, and it can finally be articulated only at the
price of a kind of liberation" (60).

18. Kingston calls the "White Tigers" fantasy a "sort of kung fu
movie parody" in her critical review of American reviews of her work
("Cultural Mis-readings" 57). I had a similar Saturday-serial fantasy in
my own girlhood, styled on a wild-west Zorro-like character. Clad
boldly in black and riding a black horse, I would valiantly fight off
desperadoes (always men) who preyed upon defenseless men, women,
and children.

19. I have drawn on the pioneering discussions of mother–daughter
ambivalence by Nancy Chodorow, Dorothy Dinnerstein, and Jane Flax,
which remain relevant despite the astute criticism levelled at them.

20. For an eloquent and persuasive discussion of truth-telling as
story-telling, see Trinh Minh-ha's "Grandma's Story" in *Woman, Native, Other*.

21. See Leslie Rabine's important reading of "Kingston's work as a
unique kind of feminine writing that in its own way fractures the logic
of opposition into a play of difference . . . [which] clarifies relations
between social and symbolic gender" (474). Also see Celeste Schenck's
discussion of the story of Ts'ai Yen as representing a "return to the
exiled mother as the source of poetry and the difference between
mother and daughter which allows this female subject to find her own
writing voice" (303).

22. Kingston broaches from a different perspective many of the
questions raised by Julia Kristeva in "Women's Time." Kristeva sees a
new generation of women whose "attitude" toward issues raised by
feminism "could be summarized as an *interiorization of the founding separation of the socio-symbolic contract*," as an "introduction of its cutting

edge into the very interior of every identity whether subjective, sexual, ideological, or so forth" (210; emphasis in original).

23. Also see Nancy K. Miller's discussion of "quipos," a system of knotting used in the Inca Empire, which she interprets as a "signature" of feminist writing (137–42).

NOTES TO CHAPTER SIX

1. Foucault's critique of the universal intellectual and of his own practices as a specific intellectual are elaborated in Paul Bove's *Intellectuals in Power,* especially in chapter 5, "Intellectuals at War: Michel Foucault and the Analytics of Power" (209–37).

2. While many on the left no doubt flinch at the misogynistic, racist, heterosexist, and monopoly-capitalistic associations that accompany the classification of people according to their being women, blacks, gays, lesbians, and workers, these analytical categories remain central to much leftist discourse. Denise Riley's deconstructive exploration of "women" is of value for unsettling that particular categorization. She points out, however, that some degree of categorization is *strategically* necessary for identity politics.

3. Jordan arranges the first essays in *On Call* in chronological order but breaks that pattern later in the text, following instead a logical order for the development and application of certain ideas. (Chapter 17, for example, was written before chapter 16 but, perhaps because it is an application of the ideas in chapter 16, appears after it in the text.) This encourages a reading of *On Call* as a narrative of ethical subject-formation.

4. These lines are from Wheatley's "Thoughts On the Works of Providence." See Jordan's discussion (92–93).

5. For a discussion of the implications for writing courses of a Foucauldian pedagogy, see Kurt Spellmeyer.

6. Also see George Yudice's important discussion of the work of specific intellectuals and of an everyday aesthetics of existence in "Marginality and the Ethics of Survival."

7. For Foucault's most extended discussion of the practice of liberty, see "The Ethic of Care for the Self as a Practice of Freedom," an interview conducted in January 1984.

BIBLIOGRAPHY

Adams, John Quincy. *Memoirs*. Ed. Charles Francis Adams. Vol. 1. Philadelphia: J. B. Lippincott, 1874.

Agee, James, and Walker Evans. *Let Us Now Praise Famous Men*. Boston: Houghton Mifflin, 1941.

Aiken, Susan Hardy. "Scripture and Poetic Discourse in *The Subjection of Women*." *PMLA* 98 (1983): 353–73.

Anderson, Charles. *The Magic Circle of Walden*. New York: Holt, Rinehart and Winston, 1968.

Armstrong, James. "Thoreau, Chastity, and the Reformers." In *Thoreau's Psychology: Eight Essays*, 123–44. Ed. Raymond Gozzi and Norman Holland. Lanham, Md.: University Press of America, 1983.

Bakhtin, M. M. "Epic and Novel." In *The Dialogic Imagination*, 3–40. Ed. Michael Holquist. Trans. Caryl Emerson and Michael Holquist. Austin: University of Texas Press, 1981.

Barson, Alfred T. *A Way of Seeing*. Amherst: University of Massachusetts Press, 1972.

Bauer, Dale M. *Feminist Dialogics: A Theory of Failed Community*. Albany: State University of New York Press, 1988.

Beecher, Catharine. *A Treatise on Domestic Economy*. [1841] Reprint, New York: Schocken Books, 1977.

Benstock, Shari. "Authorizing the Autobiographical." In *The Private Self: Theory and Practice in Women's Autobiographical Writings*, 10–33. Ed. Shari Benstock. Chapel Hill: University of North Carolina Press, 1988.

Berger, John. "Paul Strand." In *About Looking*, 41–47. New York: Pantheon, 1980.

Berlant, Lauren. "The Female Complaint." *Social Text* 19/20 (Fall 1988): 237–59.

Betts, Leonidas. "The 'Unfathomably Mysterious' *Let Us Now Praise Famous Men*." *English Journal* 59 (1970): 47, 51.

Blinde, Patricia Lin. "The Icicle in the Desert: Perspective and Form in the Works of Two Chinese-American Women Writers." *MELUS* 6 (1979): 51–71.

Bove, Paul A. *Intellectuals in Power: A Genealogy of Critical Humanism.* New York: Columbia University Press, 1986.

Bruss, Elizabeth. "Eye for I: Making and Unmaking of Autobiography in Film." In *Autobiography: Essays Theoretical and Critical,* 297–320. Ed. James Olney. Princeton: Princeton University Press, 1980.

Bryson, Norman. *Vision and Painting: The Logic of the Gaze.* New Haven: Yale University Press, 1983.

Carus, Paul. *Chinese Astrology.* Abridged from 1907 text. La Salle, Ill.: Open Court Press, 1974.

Chesnick, Eugene. "The Plot Against Fiction: *Let Us Now Praise Famous Men.*" *Southern Literary Journal* 4 (Fall 1971): 48–67.

Cheung, King-Kok. " 'Don't Tell': Imposed Silences in *The Color Purple* and *The Woman Warrior.*" *PMLA* 103 (1988): 162–74.

Chevigny, Bell Gale. *The Woman and the Myth: Margaret Fuller's Life and Writings.* Old Westbury, N.Y.: Feminist Press, 1976.

Chinard, Gilbert. "Jefferson Among the Philosophers." *Ethics* 53 (1942–43): 255–68.

Chodorow, Nancy. *The Reproduction of Mothering.* Los Angeles: University of California Press, 1978.

Cox, James M. "Recovering Literature's Lost Ground Through Autobiography." In *Autobiography: Essays Theoretical and Critical,* 121–45. Ed. James Olney. Princeton: Princeton University Press, 1980.

Davidson, Frank. "Thoreau's Hound, Bay Horse, and Turtle-Dove." *New England Quarterly* 27 (1954): 521–24.

D'Emilio, John, and Estelle Freedman. *Intimate Matters: A History of Sexuality in America.* New York: Harper and Row, 1988.

Diamond, Irene, and Lee Quinby. *Feminism and Foucault: Reflections on Resistance.* Boston: Northeastern University Press, 1988.

Dinnerstein, Dorothy. *The Mermaid and the Minotaur.* New York: Harper and Row, 1976.

Eakin, John Paul. *Fictions in Autobiography: Studies in the Art of Self-Intervention.* Princeton: Princeton University Press, 1985.

Edwards, Jonathan. *Religious Affections.* Ed. John E. Smith. Vol. 2 of *Works.* New Haven: Yale University Press, 1959.

Emerson, Ralph Waldo. *Journals and Miscellaneous Notebooks of Ralph Waldo Emerson.* Ed. Merton M. Sealts, Jr. Vol. V. Cambridge: Harvard University Press, 1965.

Evans, Walker. "James Agee in 1936." In *Let Us Now Praise Famous Men,* ix–xi. New York: Ballantine Books, 1966.

Fiering, Norman. "Benjamin Franklin And The Way To Virtue." *American Quarterly* 30 (1978): 199–223.

Flax, Jane. "The Conflict Between Nurturance and Autonomy in Mother-Daughter Relationships and Within Feminism." *Feminist Studies* 4 (1978): 171–89.

Foucault, Michel. "The Concern for Truth." In *Michel Foucault: Politics, Philosophy, Culture, Interviews and Other Writings, 1977–1984,* 255– 67. Ed. Lawrence D. Kritzman. New York: Routledge, 1988.

————"The Confession of the Flesh." In *Power/Knowledge: Selected Interviews and Other Writings, 1972–1977,* 194–228. Ed. Colin Gordon. Trans. Colin Gordon et al. New York: Pantheon, 1980.

————*Discipline and Punish: The Birth of the Prison.* Trans. Alan Sheridan. New York: Vintage, 1979.

————"The Ethic of Care for the Self as a Practice of Freedom, an Interview with Michel Foucault." In *The Final Foucault.* Ed. James W. Bernauer and David Rasmussen. Trans. J. D. Gauthier, S. J. *Philosophy and Social Criticism* 12 (1987): 112–31.

————"On the Genealogy of Ethics: An Overview of Work in Progress." In *Michel Foucault: Beyond Structuralism and Hermeneutics,* 2d ed., 229–52. Ed. Herbert L. Dreyfus and Paul Rabinow. Chicago: University of Chicago Press, 1983.

————*The History of Sexuality.* Vol. 1. Trans. Robert Hurley. New York: Vintage, 1980.

————"The Minimalist Self." In *Michel Foucault: Politics, Philosophy, Culture, Interviews and Other Writings, 1977–1984,* 3–16. Ed. Lawrence D. Kritzman. New York: Routledge, 1988.

————"Polemics, Politics, and Problemizations: An Interview with Michel Foucault." In *The Foucault Reader,* 381–390. Ed. Paul Rabinow. New York: Pantheon, 1984.

————"The Political Technology of Individuals." In *Technologies of the Self: A Seminar with Michel Foucault,* 144–62. Ed. Luthur H. Martin, Huck Gutman, and Patrick H. Hutton. Amherst: University of Massachusetts Press, 1988.

————"Power and Sex." In *Michel Foucault: Politics, Philosophy, Culture, Interviews and Other Writings,* 110–24. Ed. Lawrence D. Kritzman. New York: Routledge, 1988.

————"The Subject and Power." In *Art After Modernism: Rethinking Representation,* 417–32. Ed. Brian Wallis. New York: New Museum of Contemporary Art, 1984.

————"Technologies of the Self." In *Technologies of the Self: A Seminar with Michel Foucault,* 16–49. Ed. Luthur H. Martin, Huck Gutman, and Patrick H. Hutton. Amherst: University of Massachusetts Press, 1988.

————"Truth and Power." In *Power/Knowledge: Selected Interviews and Other Writings, 1972–1977,* 109–33. Ed. Colin Gordon. Trans. Colin Gordon et al. New York: Pantheon, 1980.

————*The Use of Pleasure.* Vol. 2 of *The History of Sexuality.* Trans. Robert Hurley. New York: Pantheon, 1985.

————"What is an Author?" In *The Foucault Reader,* 101–20. Ed. Paul Rabinow. New York: Pantheon, 1984.

————"What is Enlightenment?" In *The Foucault Reader,* 32–50. Ed. Paul Rabinow. New York: Pantheon, 1984.

Franklin, Benjamin. *Benjamin Franklin's Autobiography.* Ed. J. A. Leo Lemay and P. M. Zall. New York: Norton, 1986.

Fuller, Margaret. "Emerson's Essays." *New York Daily Tribune,* 7 December 1844. In *The Writings of Margaret Fuller.* Ed. Mason Wade. New York: Viking, 1941.

————*Woman in the Nineteenth Century.* New York: Norton, 1971.

Garber, Frederick. *Thoreau's Redemptive Imagination.* New York: New York University Press, 1977.

Gilbert, Sandra. "From *Patria* to *Matria:* Elizabeth Barrett Browning's Risorgimento." *PMLA* 99 (1984): 194–211.

Gilligan, Carol. *In a Different Voice: Psychological Theory and Women's Development.* Cambridge: Harvard University Press, 1982.

Greenblatt, Stephen. *Renaissance Self-Fashioning: From More to Shakespeare.* Chicago: University of Chicago Press, 1980.

Holaday, Woon-Ping Chin. "From Ezra Pound to Maxine Hong Kingston: Expressions of Chinese Thought in American Literature." *MELUS* 5 (1978): 15–24.

Holder, Alan. "Encounter in Alabama: Agee and the Tenant Farmer." *Virginia Quarterly Review* 42 (1966): 191–206.

Hooker, Thomas. "Meditation." In *The Puritans,* 301–6. Ed. Perry Miller and Thomas H. Johnson. New York: Harper and Row, 1963.

Hoopes, James. "Modernist Criticism and Transcendentalist Literature." *New England Quarterly* 52 (1979): 451–66.

Jaggar, Alison M. *Feminist Politics and Human Nature.* Totowa, N.J.: Rowman and Allanheld, 1983.

Jefferson, Thomas. *Notes on the State of Virginia.* Ed. William Peden. New York: Norton, 1972.

——*The Papers of Thomas Jefferson.* Ed. Julian P. Boyd. 20 vols. Princeton: Princeton University Press, 1950.

Johansen, Ruthann K. "The Sound of Jubilation: Toward An Explication of Agee's Musical Form." *Southern Quarterly* 18 (1980): 18–31.

Johnson, Barbara. "A Hound, a Bay Horse, and a Turtle Dove: Obscurity in *Walden.*" In *A World of Difference,* 49–56. Baltimore: Johns Hopkins University Press, 1989.

Jordan, June. *On Call: Political Essays.* Boston: South End Press, 1985.

Jordan, Winthrop. *White Over Black: American Attitudes Toward the Negro, 1550–1812.* New York: Norton, 1968.

Juhasz, Suzanne. "Towards a Theory of Form in Feminist Autobiography: Kate Millett's *Fear of Flying* and *Sita;* Maxine Hong Kingston's *The Woman Warrior.*" *International Journal of Women's Studies* 2 (1979): 62–75.

Kingston, Maxine Hong. "Cultural Mis-readings by American Reviewers." In *Asian and Western Writers in Dialogue,* 55–65. Ed. Guy Amirthanayagam. London: Macmillan, 1982.

——*The Woman Warrior: Memoirs of a Girlhood Among Ghosts.* New York: Alfred A. Knopf, 1977.

Kristeva, Julia. "A New Type of Intellectual: The Dissident." In *The Kristeva Reader,* 292–300. Ed. Toril Moi. Trans. Sean Hand. New York: Columbia University Press, 1986.

——"Women's Time." In *The Kristeva Reader,* 187–213. Ed. Toril Moi. Trans. Alice Jardine and Harry Blake. New York: Columbia University Press, 1986.

Leverenz, David. *Manhood and the American Renaissance.* Ithaca: Cornell University Press, 1989.

MacCannell, Juliet Flower. "Oedipus Wrecks: Lacan, Stendhal and the Narrative Form of the Real." In *Lacan and Narration: The Psychoanalytic Difference in Narrative Theory,* 910–40. Ed. Robert Con Davis. Baltimore: Johns Hopkins University Press, 1983.

MacLean, Robert. "Narcissus and the Voyeur: James Agee's *Let Us Now Praise Famous Men.*" *Journal of Narrative Technique* 11 (Winter 1981): 33–52.

Magner, Lois. "Women and the Scientific Idiom." *Signs* 4 (1978): 61–80.

Martin, Biddy. "Lesbian Identity and Autobiographical Difference[s]." In *Life/Lines: Theorizing Women's Autobiography*, 77–103. Ed. Bella Brodzki and Celeste Schenck. Ithaca: Cornell University Press, 1988.

Matthews, Richard K. *The Radical Politics of Thomas Jefferson*. Lawrence: University Press of Kansas, 1984.

Matthiessen, F. O. *American Renaissance: Art and Expression in the Age of Emerson and Whitman*. New York: Oxford University Press, 1941.

Michaels, Walter Benn. "*Walden*'s False Bottoms." *Glyph* 1 (1977): 132–49.

Miller, Nancy K. *Subject to Change*. New York: Columbia University Press, 1988.

Mitchell, W. J. T. *Iconology: Image, Text, Ideology*. Chicago: University of Chicago Press, 1986.

Moller, Mary Elkins. "Thoreau, Womankind, and Sexuality." *Emerson Society Quarterly* 22 (1976): 123–48.

Montaigne, Michel. *The Complete Essays of Montaigne*. Trans. Donald F. Frame. Stanford: Stanford University Press, 1965.

Moreau, Genevieve. *The Restless Journey of James Agee*. Trans. Miriam Kleiger and Morty Schiff. New York: William Morrow, 1977.

Neufeldt, Leonard N. *The Economist: Henry Thoreau and Enterprise*. New York: Oxford University Press, 1989.

———"The Good and the Beautiful: Thoreau's Moral-Aestheticism." *Thoreau Journal Quarterly* 12 (1980): 5–24.

Nightingale, Florence. *Cassandra*. [1869] Reprint, Old Westbury, N.Y.: Feminist Press, 1979.

Paul, Sherman. *The Shores of America*. Urbana: University of Illinois Press, 1958.

Peairs, Edith. "The Hound, the Bay Horse, and the Turtle-Dove: A Study of Thoreau and Voltaire." *PMLA* 52 (1937): 863–69.

Peden, William. "Introduction." In *Notes on the State of Virginia*, xi–xxv. New York: Norton, 1972.

Peterson, Merrill. *Thomas Jefferson and the New Nation*. New York: Oxford University Press, 1970.

Pratt, Linda Ray. "Imagining Existence: Form and History in Steinbeck and Agee." *Southern Review* 11 (1975): 84–98.

Pudaloff, Ross. "Thoreau's Composition of the Narrator: From Sexuality to Language." *Bucknell Review* 29 (1985): 121–42.

Quinby, Lee. "Thomas Jefferson: The Virtue of Aesthetics and the Aesthetics of Virtue." *American Historical Review* 87 (April 1982): 337–56.

Rabine, Leslie. "No Lost Paradise: Social Gender and Symbolic Gender in the Writings of Maxine Hong Kingston." *Signs* 12 (1987), 471–92.

Rajchman, John. "Foucault's Art of Seeing." *October* 44 (Spring 1988): 89–117.

Reising, Russell. *The Unusable Past: Theory and the Study of American Literature*. New York: Methuen, 1986.

Riley, Denise. *"Am I That Name?": Feminism and the Category of "Women" in History*. Minneapolis: University of Minnesota Press, 1987.

Robinson, David M. "Margaret Fuller and the Transcendental Ethos: *Woman in the Nineteenth Century*." *PMLA* 97 (1982): 83–98.

Rorty, Richard. *Contingency, Irony, and Solidarity*. Cambridge: Cambridge University Press, 1989.

———"The Priority of Democracy to Philosophy." In *Reading Rorty*, 279–302. Ed. Alan Malachowski. Cambridge: Basil Blackwell, 1990.

Ross, Andrew. *No Respect: Intellectuals and Popular Culture*. New York: Routledge, 1989.

Rousseau, Jean-Jacques. *Emile*. Trans. Barbara Foxley. New York: Dutton, 1974.

Schenck, Celeste. "All of a Piece: Women's Poetry and Autobiography." In *Life/Lines: Theorizing Women's Autobiography*, 281–305. Ed. Bella Brodzki and Celeste Schenck. Ithaca: Cornell University Press, 1988.

Schmidt, Jan Zlotnik. "The Other: A Study of Persona in Several Contemporary Women's Autobiographies." *CEA Critic* 43 (1981): 24–31.

Seib, Kenneth. *James Agee: Promise and Fulfillment*. Pittsburgh: University of Pittsburgh Press, 1968.

Shanley, J. Lyndon. *The Making of Walden*. Chicago: University of Chicago Press, 1957.

Sheehan, Bernard. *The Seeds of Extinction*. New York: Norton, 1973.

Sheridan, Eugene R. "Introduction." In *Jefferson's Extracts from the Gospels*. Ed. Dickinson W. Adams. Princeton: Princeton University Press, 1983.

Shloss, Carol. "The Privilege of Perception." *Virginia Quarterly Review* 56 (1980): 596–611.

Sledge, Linda Ching. "Maxine Kingston's *China Men:* The Family Historian as Epic Poet." *MELUS* 7 (1980): 3–22.

Smith, Sidonie. *A Poetics of Women's Autobiography: Marginality and the Fictions of Self-Representation.* Bloomington: Indiana University Press, 1987.

Sommer, Doris. " 'Not Just a Personal Story': Women's *Testimonios* and the Plural Self." In *Life/Lines: Theorizing Women's Autobiography,* 107–30. Ed. Bella Brodzki and Celeste Schenck. Ithaca: Cornell University Press, 1988.

Sowerby, E. Millicent. *Catalogue of the Library of Thomas Jefferson.* Vol. 2. Washington, D.C.: Library of Congress, 1953.

Spellmeyer, Kurt. "Foucault and the Freshman Writer: Considering the Self in Discourse." *College English* 51 (1989): 715–29.

Stolnitz, Jerome. " 'Beauty': Some Stages in the History of an Idea." *Journal of the History of Ideas* 22 (1961): 185–204.

Stott, William. *Documentary Expression and Thirties America.* New York: Oxford University Press, 1973.

Tagg, John. *The Burden of Representation: Essays on Photographies and Histories.* Amherst: University of Massachusetts Press, 1988.

Thoreau, Henry David. *Walden.* [1854] Reprint, Princeton: Princeton University Press, 1971.

Todorov, Tzvetan. *The Conquest of America.* Trans. Richard Howard. New York: Harper Colophon, 1984.

Trilling, Lionel. "Greatness With One Fault In It." *Kenyon Review* 4 (1942): 99–102.

Trinh Minh-ha. *Woman, Native, Other: Writing, Postcoloniality and Femininity.* Bloomington: Indiana University Press, 1989.

Ulrich, Laurel Thatcher. "Vertuous Women Found, New England Ministerial Literature, 1668–1735." In *A Heritage of Her Own,* 58–80. Ed. Nancy Cott and Elizabeth Pleck. New York: Simon and Schuster, 1979.

Urbanski, Marie Mitchell Olesen. *Margaret Fuller's Woman in the Nineteenth Century.* Westport, Conn.: Greenwood Press, 1980.

Ward, J. A. "James Agee's Aesthetic of Silence: *Let us Now Praise Famous Men.*" *Tulane Studies in English* 23 (1978): 193–206.

Welter, Barbara. "The Cult of True Womanhood: 1820–1860." *American Quarterly* 18 (1966): 151–74.

Wills, Garry. *Inventing America: Jefferson's Declaration of Independence.* Garden City, N.Y.: Doubleday, 1978.

Woodward, Kathleen. "Simone de Beauvoir: Aging and Its Discontents." In *The Private Self: Theory and Practice of Women's Autobiographical Writings,* 90–113. Ed. Shari Benstock. Chapel Hill: University of North Carolina Press, 1989.

Yudice, George. "Marginality and the Ethics of Survival." In *Universal Abandon? The Politics of Postmodernism,* 214–36. Ed. Andrew Ross. Minneapolis: University of Minnesota Press, 1988.

Zaller, Robert. "Let Us Now Praise James Agee." *Southern Literary Journal* 10 (1978): 144–54.

INDEX